JAN - - 2013

DATE DUE

			PRINTED IN U.S.A.

Greek Mythology

DON NARDO

LUCENT BOOKS

A part of Gale, Cengage Learning

GALE
CENGAGE Learning·

Detroit • New York • San Francisco • New Haven, Conn • Waterville, Maine • London

LIBRARY OF CONGRESS CATALOGING-IN-PUBLICATION DATA

Nardo, Don, 1947-
  Greek mythology / by Don Nardo.
    pages. cm. -- (Mythology and culture worldwide)
  ISBN 978-1-4205-0633-4 (hardcover)
  1. Mythology, Greek--Juvenile literature. I. Title. II. Series: Mythology and culture worldwide.
  BL783.N355 2012
  292.1'30938--dc23

                                                        2011052300

Lucent Books
27500 Drake Rd.
Farmington Hills, MI 48331

ISBN-13: 978-1-4205-0633-4
ISBN-10: 1-4205-0633-1

Printed in the United States of America
2 3 4 5 6 7 16 15 14 13 12

TABLE OF CONTENTS

Map of Ancient Greece

Family Tree of the Major Greek Gods

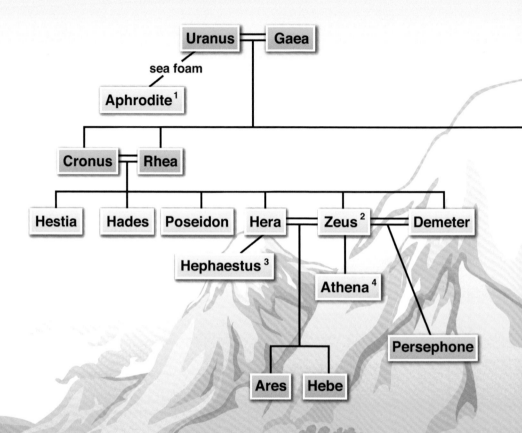

Note: Double lines joining two names indicate that these gods had offspring together. Blue shading designates the major Olympians.

1 The most common account of Aphrodite's origin says that Cronus sliced off Uranus's genitals and they fell into the sea. Foam formed around the parts and Aphrodite sprang from the foam.

2 Zeus appears several times in the tree because he had children with several different deities as well as some mortals.

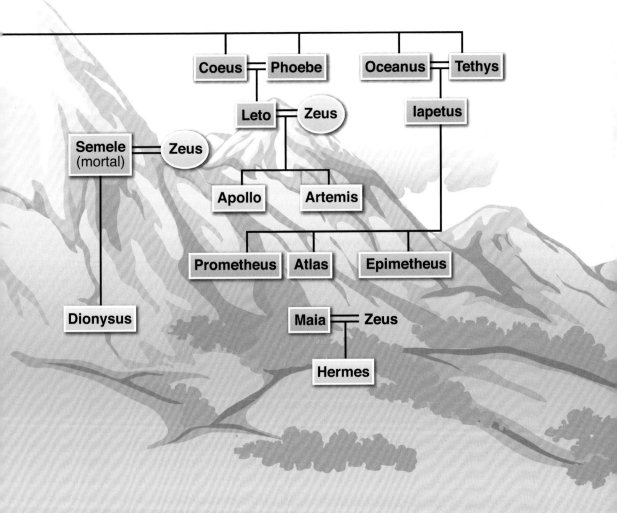

3 Some ancient sources say Hephaestus was the son of Zeus and Hera, but many others claim that Hera bore Hephaestus on her own without any union with Zeus.

4 Athena is most often said to have sprung suddenly from Zeus's head.

Major Characters in Greek Mythology

Character Name	Pronounciation	Description
Achilles	uh-KILL-eez	A great Greek warrior and the main character of Homer's *Iliad*.
Agamemnon	ag-uh-MEM-non	The leader of the Greek expedition to Troy in Homer's *Iliad*.
Aphrodite	a-froh-DY-tee	The Olympian goddess of beauty and love.
Apollo	uh-POL-oh	The Olympian god of prophecy, healing, and archery.
Athena	uh-THEE-nuh	The Olympian goddess of war and wisdom; patron deity of Athens.
Cronus	KROH-nus	Leader of the Titans, the first race of Greek gods.
Gaea	GUY-uh, or JEE-uh	The primeval spirit of the earth and the wife of Uranus.
Hector	HEK-ter	In Homer's *Iliad*, a prince of Troy and a great warrior.
Helen	HEL-en	Wife of Menealaus, king of Sparta, and lover of the Trojan prince Paris.
Heracles	HAIR-uh-kleez	Son of Zeus and Alomena; used his superhuman strength to accomplish the twelve labors.
Jason	JAY-son	Prince of Iolcos whose quest was to find the golden fleece.
Menealaus	men-uh-LAY-us	In Homer's *Iliad*, Helen's husband and Agamemnon's brother.
Odysseus	oh-DISS-ee-us	In Homer's *Iliad* and *Odyssey*, the king of Ithaca.
Oedipus	ED-uh-pus	A king of Thebes who discovers that he has killed his father and married his mother.

Orpheus	**OR-fee-us**	Son of the muse Calliope and the god Apollo who failed to save his wife, Eurydice, from the underworld.
Pandora	**Pan-DOR-uh**	First woman sent to earth by Zeus, infamous for bringing pain and suffering into the world.
Paris	**PAIR-us**	In Homer's *Iliad*, a prince of Troy who runs away with Helen, instigating the Trojan War.
Patroclus	**pa-TROH-klus**	In Homer's *Iliad*, Achilles's best friend.
Penelope	**p'NELL-uh-pee**	In Homer's *Odyssey*, Odysseus's wife.
Perseus	**PUR-see-us**	Hero who slew Medusa with help from Hermes and Athena.
Polyphemus	**pa-luh-FEE-mus**	In Homer's *Odyssey*, a giant cyclops.
Prometheus	**proh-MEE-thee-us**	The Titan who created humans and gave them fire.
Priam	**PRY-um**	The king of Troy during the Trojan War.
Rhea	**REE-uh**	A Titan, she was Cronus's wife and Zeus's mother.
Telemachus	**tel-EM-uh-kiss**	In Homer's *Odyssey*, Odysseus's son.
Theseus	**THEE-see-us**	Hero and Athenian prince who slew the Minotaur.
Uranus	**YUR-uh-niss**	The primeval spirit of the sky and the husband of Gaea.
Zeus	**ZOOSe**	The leader of the Greek Oympian gods.

Products of Ancient Imagination

A leisurely stroll through the aisles of a library or bookshop will reveal that numerous volumes about Greek mythology are on the shelves at any given moment. In fact, many thousands of books on that topic were published in the twentieth century alone. Moreover, they were written in dozens of languages and for readers of all ages. Some retell the familiar myths, injecting into them at least some element of freshness. Others study and analyze those ancient stories and the unique ancient culture that produced them with the aim of understanding both a little better than before. Still other books both retell some of the myths and examine their origins.

Yet as numerous as they are, books about the Greek myths represent only the tip of the iceberg, so to speak, of the cultural impact of these tales. Ancient Greek plays based on those myths—including the famous *Oedipus the King, Prometheus Bound,* and *Medea*—are staged over and over again, year after year, in the United States, Britain, and many other countries. New Hollywood and TV movies about Greek mythology also appear on a regular basis. Some of the better known include *Troy* (2004), *Jason and the Argonauts* (1963 and 2000), and *Clash of the Titans* (1981 and 2010). Fiction writers tell modern versions of the Greek myths in series like Percy Jackson and the Olympians, and characters from Greek mythology make appearances in the Harry Potter series. In addition, dozens of popular video games, among them *Age of Mythology, Civilization,* and *God of War,* involve mythical Greek characters and stories.

When the World Was Young

One cannot help but wonder why modern Western (European-based) civilization is so fascinated and entertained by these tales first told thousands of years ago. Part of the answer is that the myths are one of many cultural inheritances from the ancient Greeks. Indeed, through language, literature, architecture, political and scientific ideas, philosophy, and much more, the Greeks largely founded Western civilization. No less influential on this list of legacies is the surviving body of Greek myths. According to the renowned late historian Michael Grant,

> Time after time these products of ancient imagination have been used to inspire fresh creative efforts, which amount to a substantial part of our whole cultural inheritance. [Modern] writers, from tragic theater to comic strip, have continued to employ the [mythical characters] with renewed vigor. These dramatic, concrete, individual, insistently probing ancient myths [remain] clues to much in the world that does not alter.[1]

Grant's mention of "much in the world that does not alter" refers to the timeless qualities of these myths. They were created near the dawn of Western civilization, and since then many nations and peoples have come and gone. Yet the colorful, magical qualities of these stories still strongly appeal to the human imagination. The popular classics scholar Edith Hamilton wrote,

> The real interest of these myths is that they lead us back to a time when the world was young and people had a connection with the earth, with trees and seas and flowers and hills, unlike anything we ourselves can feel. When the stories were being shaped . . . little

distinction had yet been made between the real and the unreal. The imagination was vividly alive [in] that strangely and beautifully animated world.[2]

When Gods Walked the Earth

Another factor that makes that fabled world of the past so charming and alluring is that it was rumored to be a time and place when humans interacted with gods. After all, the Greek myths were closely linked to the Greeks' religious traditions, which included multiple deities having powers far beyond those of humans. Similarly, nearly all faiths, past and present, look back with fondness and reverence to a time when gods, angels, and other supernatural beings walked the earth. The Judeo-Christian Bible, Muslim Koran, and

The Acropolis in Athens. Through language, architecture, and literature, as well as political, philosophical, and scientific ideas, the ancient Greeks largely founded Western civilization.

the religious stories of India, Persia, the ancient Americas, and many other lands all have passages describing such a remarkable past era.

For that reason, many people, no matter where they live, can relate to and enjoy the ongoing retellings of the Greek myths. Because of ancient Greece's enormous legacy to Western society, however, these tales occupy a special place in the hearts of Westerners. Those extraordinary "products of ancient imagination," as Grant called them, have become deeply and forever embedded in Western literature, films, arts, and even Westerners' ways of viewing the world. Indeed, he says, the many modern versions of the Greek myths "can be claimed as the most significant of all the impacts that the [Greeks have] made upon modern thought."[3]

CHAPTER 1

Myths as Memories

The ancient Greek myths evolved in a time and place in which the Greek people's lives were relentlessly and powerfully shaped by the harsh realities of geography and nature. As the acclaimed English classics scholar C.M. Bowra put it, "Nature nursed the Greeks in a hard school."[4] Another noted historian of Greece, Sarah B. Pomeroy, elaborates:

> Greece is about the size of England . . . or the state of Alabama. [The] landscape is very rugged, with mountains covering almost 75 percent of the land. Only about 30 percent of the land can be cultivated at all [and] the mountain ranges, which are . . . quite steep and craggy, made overland travel very difficult in antiquity [ancient times], and somewhat isolated the small valleys and their people from one another. . . . The nearby Aegean [Sea], though often calm with favoring winds, could just as suddenly broil up into ferocious storms sending ships, cargo, and sailors to the bottom. . . . It is no wonder, considering the extent to which the Greeks were at the mercy of the land, sky, and sea, that the gods they worshiped were personifications of the elements and forces of nature.[5]

Indeed, the chief of the Greek gods, Zeus, was known to whip up violent storms and hurl his signature thunderbolt to and fro. Meanwhile, his brother Poseidon, lord of the seas, when aroused to anger, unleashed destructive earthquakes, storms, and floods. In one well-known myth, Zeus commands Poseidon to help him unleash floods on the earth to punish humanity for its recent failure to give the gods their proper amount of worship. As the prominent ancient Roman myth-teller and poet Ovid told it,

> Zeus's anger [was not] content with the power of his own storms, but Poseidon, his brother, aided him with additional waves. The ruler of the sea called together the rivers. [He] struck the Earth with his trident [three-pronged spear] and it trembled, and, by its motion it lay open wide paths for the waters. The overflowing rivers rushed through the open fields and carried with them both trees and, at the same time, animals and humans and even temples and their sacred chambers and statues. If any house remained standing and was able to resist the great flood without being thrown down, nevertheless the water rose higher than the roof, covering it.[6]

Natural Cycles

The turmoil and mayhem the gods caused when either fighting among themselves or punishing humans was clearly an example of using myths to explain major, frequently destructive natural events. The Greeks also had myths explaining other, less-turbulent natural phenomena, such as the changing of the seasons. More than one myth explained this natural occurrence, but one of the more well known ones asserted that the seasons were caused when the goddess of fertility and fruitfulness, Demeter, had to give up her daughter Persephone to Hades, god of the Underworld, for half of each year. The months that Persephone spends with her mother on the earth's surface are spring and summer, when plants, flowers, and crops grow and prosper. The months Persephone must remain in the Underworld, when Demeter is mourning, are fall and winter, when the plants die and the earth is cold and desolate.

This myth displays a logical attempt by people in an unscientific society to explain the existence of the seasons. It is not only imaginative and colorful, but also religious in nature. The gladness that humans feel when spring comes each year is echoed in the joy Demeter feels when reunited with her daughter again. Thus, the human race and the divine race are in a sense seen as being parallel and in synch with each other.

The Greek gods just as easily displayed other familiar human emotions besides joy. Among them were love and lust, as when Zeus has repeated affairs with goddesses and mortals alike. But Zeus has a more ethical side as well. At times he displays honor and is a champion of justice, for both gods and humans.

The gods could act as protectors of favored humans or become the enemy of a person who offended them. Such episodes involving the gods and their interactions with humans were interwoven into numerous stories passed from

This ancient Greek vase depicts the myth of Persephone spending her half year with the god Hades in the Underworld. She stayed with him during the fall and winter months and with her mother on earth in the spring and summer.

It's All Greek

For a long time scholars could not read the writings left behind by the Mycenaeans, so their true identity remained uncertain. Then, in 1952 a brilliant English amateur linguist, Michael Ventris, deciphered these writings and showed that the Mycenaeans spoke an early form of Greek.

one generation to another—the famous and familiar Greek myths.

In addition to Greece's unforgiving terrain and the residents' close and personal relationship with their gods, the Greek myths were inspired by a series of historical events that spanned several centuries. During that period, which modern experts call Greece's late Bronze Age, lasting from about 1600 to 1150 B.C., a splendid civilization arose, then collapsed, and, centuries later, an even more magnificent one, generally referred to as Classical Greece, grew up in its place. The Classical Greeks began to emerge in the 700s B.C. Between about 500 and 300 B.C., they produced such famous figures as Pericles, Herodotus, Plato, and Aristotle, as well as the world's first democracy (in Athens) and Athens's cultural golden age, in which the renowned Parthenon temple was erected.

The gap between the Bronze Age and Classical Age cultures was filled by Greece's Dark Age, which lasted almost four centuries. A time of widespread poverty and illiteracy, it was the period in which most of the major Greek myths developed. Looking at how the Bronze Age culture passed away and the Classical Greeks arose upon its wreckage after the Dark Age helps to shed light on the unique character of these myths.

Greece's Bronze Age

In brief, modern scholars think that some, and perhaps many, of the Greek myths were distorted memories of real people and events from Greece's late Bronze Age. In that period, a culturally advanced people now called the Minoans (who did not speak Greek) built magnificent palace-centers on the large Mediterranean island of Crete and on nearby smaller islands in the Aegean Sea. With their large fleets of ships, the Minoans dominated the Aegean region, both economically and culturally.

In fact, for a long time the Minoans exerted a strong cultural influence on the Mycenaeans, who dwelled on the Greek mainland and spoke an early version of Greek. The mainlanders also erected large palaces; however, these were smaller and less sophisticated than the Minoan versions. It is possible that for an undetermined period the Mycenaeans were politically, as well as culturally, dominated by the Minoans, although this remains unproven. What is more certain is that the mainlanders eventually overran the Minoans and their sphere of influence. The Mycenaeans swept down on them between 1500 and 1450 B.C. The mainlanders took over Crete and the nearby islands, and the surviving Minoans now became their subjects.

Mycenaean Prosperity and Collapse

The two centuries following the Minoans' defeat witnessed the height of Mycenaean power and prosperity. The Mycenaeans took over trades routes in the Aegean and eastern Mediterranean that had been the realm of the Minoans. The new lords of Crete also periodically raided the coast of Anatolia (what is now Turkey). Toward the end of this period, an alliance of Mycenaean kings and their armies may have captured and burned the prosperous city of Troy, on Anatolia's northwestern coast.

The legendary eighth-century B.C. Greek storyteller Homer told about such an event in his epic poem the *Iliad*. Moreover, evidence uncovered in Troy's ruins shows that the city did undergo a siege in about 1220 B.C. This is the period in which the mythical Trojan War supposedly occurred.

It remains uncertain, however, that this was the siege described by Homer. For that matter, it has yet to be proven that the war depicted in the *Iliad* ever actually took place. Nevertheless, most of the myths recorded by the Classical Greeks derived from the Age of Heroes, their name for their late Bronze Age, which coincided with the age of Mycenaean prosperity. Experts think it is feasible that faint, imprecise memories of some famous Mycenaeans and their deeds were handed down as legends to later generations of Greeks.

A view of the main cemetery at Mycenae, lying near the ruins of the palace. For two centuries following the defeat of the Minoans, the Mycenaeans ruled the eastern Mediterranean and Aegean Seas.

What made the Mycenaeans go from a vital, prosperous people to mere memories and the stuff of legends was the sudden and catastrophic collapse of their kingdoms. In about 1200 B.C. or shortly thereafter, the Aegean sphere, as well as many parts of the Middle East, underwent tremendous upheaval. Most of the major Mycenaean strongholds were sacked and burned, never to be rebuilt. Archaeologists and other experts have proposed a number of theories to explain this turmoil. They include civil conflicts, ruined economies caused by a disruption of farming and trade, and the invasions of warlike peoples from southeastern Europe.

Into the Realm of Legend

Whatever the cause or causes of the catastrophe, it brought the Bronze Age to a crashing halt. Greek civilization rather suddenly entered a period of cultural, political, and material decline. No longer inhabited and maintained, the palace-citadels at Mycenae and other mainland sites began to decay, while literacy, record keeping, artistic skills, and other factors that had supported Bronze Age society were lost. Besides the ruined palaces, all that remained were memories of the powerful folk who had lived in them.

These memories became increasingly dim and exaggerated over time and blended with ancient beliefs until they were transformed into colorful, romantic fables of a time when heroes, monsters, and gods roamed the land. For this reason, Greeks in later centuries saw their dim past in mythical rather than historical terms. They idolized the

Map of the Minoan and Mycenaean Civilizations circa 1600 to 1150 B.C.

culture of the Age of Heroes, in large part because it had been exactly that—heroic. In Bowra's well-chosen words, they

> cherished legends of that resplendent past, and with the longing admiration which men feel for a greatness which they cannot recover or rival, the Greeks saw in this lost society something heroic and superhuman, which embodied an ideal of what men should be and do and suffer. Their imaginations, inflamed by ancient stories of vast undertakings and incomparable heroes, of gods walking on the earth as friends of men . . . formed a vision of a heroic world which they cherished as one of their most precious possessions.[7]

Thus, Greece's splendid Bronze Age civilization passed into the realm of legend during the Dark Age, which lasted from about 1150 to roughly 800 or 750 B.C. During those years, Greeks everywhere more or less forgot their heritage and began to identify themselves only with the particular valley or island where they lived. This marked the birth of the separate, fiercely independent city-states that would later dominate Classical Greece.

Yet although the Minoan-Mycenaean world no longer existed, the tales of its heroes and their exploits continued to pass by word of mouth from one generation to the next. Over time those stories about the marvelous Age of Heroes became progressively longer, more complex, and larger than life. Finally, some became epics; that is, majestic works told in verse (like songs or poems) and dealing with major, serious themes, such as life, death, and heroism. No one in the Dark Age knew how to read or write. So roving minstrels or bards, known as *aoidoi* (ah-ee-DEE), memorized these stories and recited them in villages and towns across the Greek sphere.

At first, the minstrels likely told and retold dozens of epic tales, including some that were eventually lost and forgotten. Eventually, however, a handful of stories emerged as the most widely known and important. One of the storytellers, who was destined to become a literary immortal, focused on two of these epics. He memorized them word

A Myth Comes to Life

One of the more famous Greek myths involves the Labyrinth, a maze-like underground structure on the island of Crete. In the story, a monster half-man and half-bull—the Minotaur—lived in the maze until the Athenian hero Theseus slew it. The Labyrinth remained a fable until Englishman Arthur Evans began excavating the low, broad mound of Kephala, near Crete's northern coast, in 1900. Rumors were that this was the site of the legendary ancient city of Knossos, whose ruler supposedly maintained the Labyrinth. It became clear to Evans that extensive ruins lay just beneath the surface of the mound, and he turned out to be right. The remains of an ancient Minoan palace covering more than three acres steadily came to light. The palace was extremely complex, with hundreds of rooms arranged in an asymmetric fashion, and Evans realized that the palace itself had inspired the myth of the Labyrinth. Since then, a number of scholars have proposed that the image of the monstrous Minotaur was a garbled memory of Minoan priests who wore bull-masks while conducting religious rituals.

Englishman Arthur Evans discovered the ruins of the palace of Knossos in Crete in 1900, seen here in a reconstruction. Evans realized that the palace itself had inspired the myth of the Labyrinth.

for word, recited them repeatedly, and made some brilliant, effective additions to them. This genius's name was Homer. The place and time of his birth are uncertain. But the best guess of both ancient and modern scholars is that he grew up on the Aegean island of Chios (KHEE-os) sometime in the late 800s or early 700s B.C.

The two oral epics Homer worked on so diligently are the *Iliad* and the *Odyssey*. The *Iliad* takes place in the last year of the fabled war between the Greeks and Trojans. It tells how the brave and proud Greek warrior Achilles quarreled with the leader of the expedition, Agamemnon, and

During Greece's Dark Age roving minstrels or bards memorized stories and recited them in villages, towns, and homes throughout Greece. They kept the myths alive.

refused to fight. Later Achilles changed his mind and reentered the fray, with dramatic, bloody results. The *Odyssey* begins after Troy's fall and traces the ten-year-long adventures of another leader of the Greek expedition, Odysseus.

The *Iliad* and *Odyssey* were the first major examples of Western literature. The Classical Greeks and, later, the Romans and other ancient peoples judged them as true masterpieces, a reputation that has remained intact ever since. For the Greeks in particular, they were more than just brilliant literary pieces. In their eyes they were national epics with profound social influences and impacts. Indeed, in Greece Homer's epics became vital sources of literary, artistic, moral, educational, and political instruction, along with practical wisdom.

Human Beings Writ Large

Through his epic poems, Homer also significantly shaped the Classical Greek religion and some of its myths about the gods and their relationships, which emerged in the Dark Age and a century or so following it. Indeed, the chief players in both religion and mythology were the gods. Homer made thousands of references to them in his epics, describing how they looked, felt, acted, and interacted with humans. Along with the poet Hesiod's lesser epics, the *Iliad* and *Odyssey* gave the Greeks a glimpse of the superbeings who were thought to control the universe.

This peek into the world of the divine revealed that the Greek gods looked and acted like people. In modern terms, they were anthropomorphic, meaning they had human forms and attributes. Picturing the gods this way no doubt made what might have been distant, mysterious, irrational forces much more approachable, understandable, and rational. Historian Michael Grant remarks,

> One of the most distinctive features of Greek religion . . . was its anthropomorphism, uniquely developed among the major religions of the world. These gods and goddesses are human beings writ large, because the Greeks, with their lively, dramatic, and plastic [flexible] sense, were so conscious of the potential of men and women that they could not imagine the deities in any other shape.[8]

One reason that the Classical Greeks envisioned their gods in human form was that they viewed the human body as the most beautiful of nature's creations. It made no sense to them that the gods would have one form and humans another. Instead, it seemed more natural, even inevitable, that those deities would possess the most attractive of all possible forms, since, after all, they existed at nature's pinnacle. Following from this logic, humans must have gained human form because the gods made them in their own image. This was reflected in one of the popular Greek myths about the early god Prometheus. Zeus gave him the task of creating the human race, and he chose to make these new beings look like himself.

Yet all Greeks knew that no matter how much the gods resembled them, or, more properly, how much they resembled the gods, one factor would

First Edition, 500 B.C.

It remains unknown when Homer's *Iliad* and *Odyssey* were first written down. One theory suggests it happened in Athens in the late 500s B.C. In this view, the city's leader, Pisistratus, ordered the epics to be committed to writing so that his city could claim it had the only written versions of Homer's masterworks.

This bust of the god Hermes dates from the fifth century B.C. The Greeks believed their gods were human in form and had human attributes.

always make them separate and unequal. The fifth-century B.C. poet Pindar, stated it well. "Single is the race, single of men and gods," he said. "From a single mother we both draw breath. But a difference of power in everything keeps us apart."⁹ Indeed, lurking beneath the surface of Greek religion, and frequently depicted in myths, was the reality that the gods could overpower or destroy even the strongest human in an instant.

Those myths about the gods proved to be an important unifying factor among the Classical Greeks, who saw their local city-states as tiny, separate, and competing nations. The residents of all these cities, although rivals and at times enemies, all considered themselves descended from the special men and women who had long ago walked among the gods. So the notion that all Greeks were kin beneath the surface was widely accepted.

The gods who populated the world depicted in the Greek myths were divided into various groups. One group consisted of the first race of divine beings—the Titans. A second group featured the major deities known as the "Olympians," so named because they supposedly dwelled atop Mount Olympus, in northern Greece. According to mythology, the Olympians, led by the sky god Zeus, defeated the Titans in a great war in the remote past. There were also numerous minor gods and goddesses who made nature seemingly come alive with human-like entities.

Greek religion was largely about people's attempts to honor, please, and satisfy these deities. The hope was that such activities would allow a person or community to get into the good graces of one or more gods. Among the basics of Greek worship were sacrifice (making offerings to the gods) and prayer; open-air altars on which the sacrifices were performed; temples (at first of wood, later of stone), each dedicated to a specific god; cult images (statues) of the gods, usually resting inside the temples; and public religious festivals to honor the gods.

Explaining How Things Came to Be

Such sacred rituals and objects are routinely depicted in the myths the Classical Greeks inherited from the Age of Heroes. Some myths were obvious attempts to explain how some of these rituals of worship got started in the first place. A good example is one of the many legendary tales about the ruler of the gods, Zeus. In it, Prometheus, who has long resented Zeus for being arrogant and bossy, is expected to present the chief deity with a gift. Trying to trick the more powerful god, Prometheus presents him with an ox made up only of bones covered by a layer of fat and keeps the meat for himself and some other gods.

Despite Prometheus's attempted ruse, Zeus immediately realizes that he has been deceived. For the time being, however, he accepts the gift, all the while plotting in his mind that he will get his revenge on Prometheus later. Nevertheless, his acceptance of the bones and fat sets a precedent. Thereafter, Prometheus's creations—people—will abide by the tradition of removing the bones and fat from sacrificial animals and burning them as an offering to the gods. (Their reasoning was that the smoke from these burned animal parts rose up to nourish and thereby to satisfy a god or gods.)

Other Greek myths illustrated the divine wrath that might ensue when people either failed to take part in such traditional worship or otherwise disrespected the gods. A well-known example is the myth of the Theban woman Niobe, who had seven sons and seven daughters. As the story begins, a Theban priestess calls on a group of local women to worship the goddess Leto, mother of the powerful twin deities Apollo and Artemis. "Women of Thebes," the priestess says, "gather at Leto's temple and offer her and her two children sacred incense and your prayers, and bind your hair with laurel. This Leto, through me, commands."[10]

While the women are praying at the temple, Niobe happens by. She insults Leto, saying that she has only two children, while Niobe has fourteen, and urges the women to stop wasting time worshipping a goddess who is not as accomplished as Niobe herself. When Leto hears of this incident, she is indeed insulted. Soon her enraged offspring, Apollo and Artemis, travel to Thebes and punish Niobe severely for her impudence. The two gods end up killing all fourteen of her children.

Another group of myths shows what could happen when humans and gods not only respected each other but also worked together to achieve a mutually beneficial goal. Typical of these stories are those that show intrepid heroes slaying tyrants and/or monsters with the aid of various gods. For example, in the famous myth of the hero Perseus, the hero endeavors to find and slay the hideous creature Medusa. Once a normal human woman, she had been changed into a monster by a goddess as a punishment. Perseus knows that even if he can find Medusa, confronting her will be risky because part of the divine curse placed on her causes anyone who gazes at her to turn into stone.

In the myth of Prometheus Zeus exacts revenge on Prometheus by chaining him to a rock on Mount Caucasus where each day an eagle eats his liver only to have it regenerated each night.

Fortunately for the young hero, he receives help from two of the leading gods. Hermes, the messenger god, gives him the information he needs to find the monster. Then, the goddess of wisdom and war, Athena, provides Perseus with a shield with a surface so polished that it acts like a mirror. She tells the man that as he approaches Medusa he should look only at her image in the shield. That way he will not gaze directly at her and turn to stone. Using these gifts from the gods, Perseus manages to find and kill Medusa. Several other familiar myths depict the gods aiding human heroes.

The ruins of the Sanctuary of Athena, among several ancient temples at the sacred site of Delphi, in central Greece. Delphi was also home to the Temple of Apollo, where people from all over Greece came to hear the words of the famous oracle.

There are also a number of myths about wars, such as the Trojan War, and epic quests, such as Odysseus's ten-year search for his home, in which the Greek deities frequently intervene. Even in the few myths in which the gods do not make a physical appearance, their presence is felt through characters talking about them, praying to them, and consulting their oracles. The latter were priestesses thought to be mediums between the divine beings and humans. The famous oracle at Delphi (in central Greece), for instance, supposedly relayed messages from Apollo to religious pilgrims who came to his temple to ask him questions about their problems or about future events.

One of the more compelling myths in which the gods do not physically appear is the famous tale of Oedipus. When

he was a young man, an oracle claimed that he would someday kill his father and marry his mother. Desperate to avoid this awful fate, he leaves his home and parents and heads for the faraway city of Thebes. On his way there an old man he meets on the road gives him trouble, so he slays him. Reaching Thebes, Oedipus kills a monster that has been terrorizing the city, and the Thebans show their gratitude by making him king. He marries the wife of the recently deceased king, and they have several children.

Eventually, however, Oedipus discovers that the parents he left behind years before had not been his real parents but rather a couple that had adopted him; moreover, the man he killed on the road had been both the Theban king and his real father. That meant that the woman he had married was his biological mother, which meant that the oracle's prediction had come true in spite of his attempts to thwart it.

In this highly dramatic story the gods, though not physically seen, are ever-present in the background. Several oracles are consulted during the course of the myth, and in each case divine guidance is offered. Moreover, at one point Thebes is struck by a crippling plague, which turns out to have been sent by the gods to punish Oedipus for his sins. Eventually, when Oedipus learns the truth, in his agony he blinds himself and begins wandering around the countryside as a wretched beggar. Once again the gods' unseen presence and will are felt as they decide to forgive Oedipus and whisk him away into their heavenly realm.

A Longing for the Divine

Thus, as these few examples show, the vast majority of Greek myths were to one degree or another about the gods and people's attempts to understand and connect with them. This attainment of an understanding of the divine will and intent, when it occurred, was seen to make the worshipper wiser and more likely to receive divine favor. But it did not necessarily make the worshipper a more righteous or moral person, as is common in modern monotheistic faiths such as Christianity and Judaism. Unlike the members of those religions, the Greeks had no divinely given ethical or moral

Excavating the Real Troy

Early modern scholars assumed that Troy had been a legendary town until its very real ruins came to light at a site called Hisarlik, in northwestern Turkey, in the late nineteenth century. Historian Peter Connolly briefly tells about the initial excavations.

Troy was discovered by an amateur archaeologist, Heinrich Schliemann, in 1870. He found several towns each built on the ruins of the previous one. At the second level up he discovered signs of burning and concluded that this was Homer's Troy. In 1882 Schliemann was joined by a professional archaeologist, Wilhelm Dörpfeld, and the excavating was soon left to him. Dörpfeld identified nine successive towns on the site and was able to show that Homer's Troy was between the sixth and seventh levels. Dörpfeld's findings were checked by an American expedition between 1932 and 1938. They agreed with his findings but improved techniques enabled them to identify no less than 30 different levels of occupation.

Peter Connolly. *The Legend of Odysseus.* New York: Oxford University Press, 1989, p. 46.

rules like the Ten Commandments or the precepts of Jesus's Sermon on the Mount.

Similarly, with occasional exceptions, the Greeks did not view the gods as role models for right or good behavior. In fact these deities more often than not misbehaved or acted in decidedly *un*ethical ways. There *were* some aspects of the gods' personalities that people might sometimes emulate. For instance, in some myths Zeus appears as a champion of justice; however, his sense of justice was inconsistent because in some myths he acts justly and in others he does not. He and his fellow gods greatly impressed the Greeks. But what awed them the most about these deities was not their moral compass but their power to control nature, perform heroic deeds, and affect human destiny. Importantly, this attitude toward the divine profoundly influenced the plots and outcomes of most Greek myths.

Ongoing attempts to understand and gain the good graces of the gods preoccupied the Greeks throughout their long history in both worship and everyday life. Edith Hamilton noted, "The Greeks from the earliest mythologists on, had a perception of the divine" that the gods represented and embodied. "Their longing for them was great enough to make them never give up laboring to see them clearly."[11] Today, long after the ancient Greeks have perished from the earth, people are still longing for and laboring to comprehend the forces that control nature and the world.

CHAPTER 2

Stories About Creation

L ike peoples in all times and places, the Greeks yearned to understand how the world came to be and to know where humans and their societies came from. They had no organized sciences of archaeology and anthropology to investigate the mysteries of human origins. So they turned instead to myths.

A number of ancient sources told or described the myths that depicted the origins of the universe, gods, and humans. Of those sources, some belonged to the so-called Epic Cycle. This collection of epic poems described mythical events from the universe's inception to the close of the Age of Heroes (Greece's late Bronze Age). Unfortunately for modern scholars and readers, none of these works have survived intact. In fact, only about 120 lines from the Epic Cycle still exist, but scholars know generally what the lost epics contained because of summaries and descriptions of them in the works of later ancient writers.

Probably the most comprehensive and important of those vanished works was the *Titanomachy* (Tie-TAHN-uh-mock-ee, meaning "War of the Titans"). It told about the emergence of the first race of gods, the Titans, and their momentous battle against the Olympian gods led by Zeus. As luck would have it, the eighth-century B.C. Greek poet

Hesiod included a large amount of material from the *Titanomachy* in his own epic, the *Theogony* ("Lineage of the Gods"), which *has* survived. Later Greek writers, notably Aeschylus and other Classical playwrights, also mined the Epic Cycle's stories for some of their plots and characters.

Thus, the Greek creation stories have been pieced together from a patchwork of ancient works. No single, universally accepted version of how the universe came to be existed in ancient Greece. Instead, there were a few competing versions that were similar overall but different in their details. Besides Hesiod's collection of myths about the creation, there was one described in *The Birds,* a comic play by the fifth-century B.C. Athenian playwright Aristophanes. A third important group of creation stories appears in the *Metamorphoses,* a large collection of Greek and Roman myths compiled by the first-century B.C. Roman poet Ovid. He incorporated ideas about nature and the universe proposed by Greek scientists during the centuries following Hesiod's death. Of these somewhat varied versions, Hesiod's is today generally viewed as the classic one, in part because it is the oldest. But which version was most widely accepted by the Greeks living in any given ancient period remains unknown.

Order Out of Chaos

In Hesiod's colorful, eventful tale of how the universe came to be, long before humans and even the gods existed there was nothing but a huge, formless, swirling mass of material. In the words of the great scholar and storyteller W.H.D. Rouse, "The seeds or beginnings of all things were mixed up together in a shapeless mass, all moving about in all directions."[12] This disorganized mass was called Chaos. Vast ages of unknown length came and went, and Chaos remained, unchanging. Then, in a way no one has ever been able to discern or explain, two vast forces appeared within Chaos—Night and Erebus. Both were as dark as a moonless night, totally silent, and seemingly endless. Their purpose, if any, was mysterious, and they seemed merely to exist.

More eons elapsed, until without warning a mystifying combination of natural force and thinking being emerged

This frieze at Delphi depicts a scene from a great battle between the gods and giants.

from the darkness. This strange life force came to be called Eros, or Love. In a way only he comprehended, Eros brought order into the cosmos (the Greek word for the universe). Because the force of love is a kind of attraction, it has a tendency to make things move toward one another and come together. In modern terms, that force is called gravity. The early Greeks did not know the reasons for the real natural force we call gravity. But they did sense, in a rudimentary display of logic, that such a force must exist. So following the religious traditions of their time, they gave it a name—Eros—and a human-like intelligence.

Thanks to his ability to make things come together, therefore, Eros allowed the disordered pieces of matter floating about in the dark to combine. The heavier elements steadily settled out and became the earth, while the lighter parts drifted upward and became the sky. The region lying beneath the earth, called Tartarus (the Underworld), stayed dark and scary. But above it Eros let loose light, whose bright, warm rays fell upon the earth and the heavens for the first time.

This opening section of the Greek creation myth hinted at something important about the way the Greeks viewed nature and the world. Namely, they did not envision a divine being creating the universe. Chaos, with its many fragmented, disordered elements, or "seeds," already existed before any deities entered the picture. Even when Eros appeared, he did not create anything; rather, he made already existing materials come together and begin to fall into logical order. In a way, he corresponds to the natural changes taking place over time that cause increasingly complex systems to develop.

Thus, the Greeks broke with the earlier creation stories of the neighboring Middle East in a crucial way. The peoples of Mesopotamia (ancient Iraq), the ancient Hebrews, and others envisioned the creation as the conscious work of a god or gods. In contrast, the Greek view of creation was, on its most basic level, more scientific than spiritual. It is not surprising, therefore, that a little more than a century after Hesiod's time, the Greeks began proposing the first scientific concepts. These held that natural laws, not supernatural beings, made the universe tick. In this way, some Greek myths reflected the unique, increasingly rational thinking of their tellers.

That sort of thinking is also reflected in an important section of the creation myths in which nature gives rise to the divine instead of the other way around. Even before the appearance of Eros, according to Hesiod, an enormous conscious spirit inhabiting the earth suddenly awoke. Her name was Gaea (or Gaia), who would later come to be called Mother Earth. She apparently longed to have a mate, so she proceeded to create one. In the sky, as a result of her influence, another immense spirit, Uranus, or Father Heaven, emerged. Wasting no time, Gaea and Uranus joined together and from their union sprang a big brood of children. As Rouse points out, this assorted assembly of siblings

> began with monsters, but they improved as they went on. Among the monsters were three, with fifty heads apiece, and a hundred hands. Their names were Cottos, Gyas, and Braireos. Three others were named the Cyclopes [SY-cloh-peez] . . . and each Cyclops had one huge eye in the middle of his forehead, with one huge and bushy eyebrow above it.[13]

Next, Gaea and Uranus generated the first race of gods, the Titans, each of whom had one head, two arms, two legs and two eyes—in other words what would later be called human form. Each Titan was a good deal larger and far more powerful than any human, however. The strongest of the Titans, who also happened to be the youngest, was Cronus (or Cronos). This brutish being took his sister Rhea as his mate.

Troubles with Children

In human terms, Gaea and Uranus were anything but typical parents. Yet just like human mothers, Gaea dearly loved her children, even the disfigured Hundred-Handers and Cyclopes. In contrast, Uranus, who was somewhat dimwitted and paranoid, hated and distrusted his offspring. He particularly disliked the six monstrous ones. Worried that they might attack and injure him, he ambushed them one by one and locked them away in deep, dark Tartarus.

When Gaea heard what her mate had done, she became "enraged at the maltreatment of her children," famous myth-teller Edith Hamilton writes. The great spirit of the earth persuaded the bold and strong Titan Cronus to rebel against and punish his father. Almost immediately, he attacked Uranus and with a sickle-like blade sliced off his genitals. Then, Hamilton continues, "a race of giants sprang up from [Uranus's] blood."[14]

Cronus won the fight and cast his still-bleeding father down into the depths of Tartarus. Now in charge of the universe, Cronus started having offspring of his own with his mate, Rhea. As his first child was nearing birth, however, he began to have second thoughts. Maybe, he speculated, his sons and daughters would end up turning on him, just as he had turned on his own father. To prevent such a scenario, when that first child arrived, Cronus seized it and swallowed it whole. (It did not die because, like the other gods, it was immortal, but for the moment it was doomed to live and grow within its father's huge body.)

Rhea Saves Zeus

Cronus swallowed the next four children Rhea birthed in the same manner. Like Gaea, Rhea loved her offspring and was horrified at their unjustified, grisly fate. So when she

Hesiod and the Muses

In the opening section of his epic poem, the Theogony, *the Greek farmer-writer Hesiod called upon the divine muses to inspire him, saying,*

Hail, daughters of Zeus! Give me sweet song to celebrate the holy race of gods who live forever, sons of starry Heaven and Earth, and gloomy Night, and salty Sea. Tell [me] how the gods and earth arose at first, and rivers and the boundless swollen sea and shining stars, and the broad heaven above, and how the gods divided up their wealth and how they shared their honors, how they first

In writing his Theogony *ancient Greek writer Hesiod called upon the divine muses to inspire him.*

captured Olympus with its many folds. Tell me these things, Olympian Muses, tell from the beginning, which first came to be?

Hesiod. *Theogony.* In *Hesiod, the Homeric Hymns, and Homerica.* Translated by H.G. Evelyn-White. Cambridge, MA: Harvard University Press, 1982, p. 26.

felt a sixth child stirring within her, she came up with a daring plan. When the baby, named Zeus (whom the Romans would later call Jupiter), was born, she hid him from her husband. In the child's place she wrapped a big stone in a blanket and handed it to Cronus. The king of the Titans, who was almost as mentally dense as his own father, was easily fooled. He quickly gulped down the stone and, satisfied with himself, fell asleep. (Later, the Classical Greeks found a rock they thought to be the one that Cronus had swallowed. Called the *omphalos* ["navel"], it was long on display at the great religious center at Delphi, which they believed to mark the center of the world.)

Having deceived her abhorrent husband, Rhea set the rest of her scheme in motion. She carried Zeus away to a cave on the island of Crete and there placed him in the care of two nymphs (minor nature goddesses).

It is only natural to wonder why Rhea chose Crete, and why the divine infant grew up in a cave. The answer is that the Classical Greek myths were riddled with images, characters, and events borrowed from the Bronze and Dark ages. It was in the Dark Age, after all, that most of the myths of the Classical Greeks developed.

In the Bronze Age, Crete had been the homeland of the Minoans. Archaeologists have shown that their ancestors lived in caves on that island. Once they started living in houses, they converted the caves into cemeteries, and eventually those same caves became places of worship and therefore sacred. According to scholar Rodney Castleden, these caves still have a "mysterious and other-worldly atmosphere." He adds, "They are places apart, like no other."

How the Greeks Saw Their Gods

Classical scholar Jacqueline de Romilly here explains how Homer portrayed the Greek gods in his epic poems. This vision of those deities was vital to the later Greeks, whose overall conception of the gods came mainly from Homer.

[H]omer] imagined the gods as living on Mt. Olympus, or simply in the sky. Their king and father was Zeus; but each had his or her own distinct personality. The poet imagines their relations with one another as those that might exist in a small human kingdom. . . . Like men, these gods have passions [that] often lead them to mingle with men, sometimes in their proper shapes, sometimes in disguise. They have their friends and their enemies. . . . With all these characteristics, the Homeric gods are not merely anthropomorphic but "human" in the extreme, with all the failings the word implies. Yet they are also radically different from men, for they are immortal and enjoy superhuman powers. [The gods] transform themselves freely; and they transform men as well, making them old or beautiful at will. . . . Homeric man is always afraid that a god may be present to thwart him, [yet] the close ties between gods and mortals can also lead to a kind of affectionate familiarity—at least in the *Odyssey*. If Odysseus is hounded by Poseidon's anger, he is just as constantly helped by Athena, who is always acting in his behalf, either among the gods, or in Ithaca, or wherever he is.

Jacqueline de Romilly. *A Short History of Greek Literature*. Chicago: University of Chicago Press, 1985, pp. 13–14.

Indeed, he notes, they are "places where deities might yet dwell."[15] The cultural memory of praying to gods thought to dwell in the recesses of Cretan caves may well have inspired the later myth of Zeus's childhood in those caves.

The Titanomachy

It did not take Zeus long to grow to adulthood. While he was still living in Crete, his mother informed him about his siblings' gruesome fate, and he began plotting a way to free them. When he was ready, the handsome young deity departed the island and acquired some extremely strong medicine. Then, secretly, he slipped it into Cronus's food. It was not long before the chief Titan started throwing up. Out came the stone that Rhea had years before substituted for Zeus, after which Cronus went on a veritable vomiting jag. One by one, the five children he had long ago swallowed burst out of his spasm-wracked body. Now grown into adults, like Zeus, they were Poseidon (the Roman Neptune), Demeter (Ceres), Hestia (Vesta), Hera (Juno), and Hades (Pluto or Dis).

Zeus's brothers and sisters were glad to be free of their putrid prison and equally happy to meet the long-lost sibling who had saved them. But at that moment there was no time for a family reunion. The enraged Cronus was gathering the other Titans to fight his liberated offspring. Soon an immense battle raged across the earth and heavens. Later, the Greeks would call it the Titanomachy, or "Battle of the Titans." For a long time Zeus and his brothers and sisters did their best to gain some sort of advantage in the fight. Fortunately for them, a few Titans came over to their side, including Prometheus, whose name means "forethought."

This enormous battle was only one example of major strife—sieges, military campaigns, duels, murders, and conflict in general—in Greek mythology. Among the many others, one of the most famous is the Trojan War, part of which Homer told about in his great epic the *Iliad*. That conflict included not only battles between Greeks and Trojans, but also rivalry among various gods who backed one side or the other.

A particularly clear-cut example of mythical violence and conflict appears in the several stories about the Athenian national hero Theseus. Son of Athens's early legendary king Aegeus (for whom the Aegean Sea was named), he was a gallant warrior who constantly used his fighting skills to defend or otherwise benefit his homeland. (In the Age of Heroes, Athens and other Greek "cities" were small kingdoms ruled by monarchs like Aegeus.) On the way to Athens to meet his father, for example, Theseus challenged, defeated, and killed some notorious criminals who had been mugging and killing Athenian travelers.

Not long afterward, the young man traveled to Crete on behalf of his nation and fought and slew the Minotaur. That heinous creature, which was half-man and half-bull, had been devouring Athenian hostages kept by the cruel king of the

This Greek amphora depicts Theseus slaying the Minotaur. He later became king of Athens and defeated the Amazons.

Cretan city of Knossos (NOS-us). Still later, Aegeus died and Theseus took his place on the Athenian throne. One of the new ruler's first duties was to defend the city from an attack by the Amazons, a legendary tribe of warrior women who dwelled near the Black Sea. In a large-scale battle that raged inside and outside of Athens, Theseus and his soldiers delivered the female invaders a major defeat.

This frequent depiction in the myths of kingdoms and city-states at war plainly reflected an identical pattern of violence and military strife in the real world of the ancient Greeks. Like the peoples, cities, and kingdoms described in the myths, the Greeks were highly territorial. This stemmed in part from the fact that throughout ancient times there was never a single, unified Greek country like the modern nation of Greece. Rather, at any given time the Greek sphere was a patchwork of no fewer than dozens and at times as many as hundreds of separate political states, each of which viewed itself as an independent, sovereign nation. These states jealously guarded their borders and interests and were quick to become embroiled in battles and wars. (In fact, the inability of the Greeks to achieve lasting and meaningful unity was the chief factor in Greece's political decline in the second and first centuries B.C.) To the Greeks, therefore, the bloody war fought between the Titans and Zeus's forces was neither surprising nor distressing.

The Olympians Take Charge

After ten long years of combat in that devastating divine conflict, the tide turned in favor of one side. With the aid of the Hundred-Handers and Cyclopes, whom Prometheus had freed from Tartarus, Zeus and his followers won the war. They dealt with their defeated opponents harshly. Cronus and the Titans who had fought alongside him ended up in gloomy Tartarus. There, they could not escape because Zeus appointed as their jailors three creatures that absolutely terrified them—the Hundred-Handers.

Having prevailed over the first race of gods, the second divine race took over and refurbished the war-ravaged world. The Classical Greeks were well aware that the new

Athena's "Birth"

According to legend, Athena burst forth from the head of her father, Zeus, clad in full armor. That outfit, befitting her role as goddess of war, included the famous aegis, a breastplate (or in some accounts a shield) bearing the face of a monster.

and better world that emerged in this part of the creation myths was the product of major rebellions. First, Cronus had revolted against his own father, Uranus. Then Zeus and his siblings had risked all by rebelling against the old order of the Titans.

This theme of rebellion as a mechanism, or tool, for helping to bring about a fair, more ordered, and/or more civilized society was common in Greek mythology. Often in these stories, the perceived need to rebel is motivated by concern for the suffering of an individual or group. In Zeus's case, the concern was for his brothers and sisters who had been languishing in the dark recesses of Cronus's belly. Freeing them ended their suffering. Also, the new divine order that emerged after the war in heaven was more ordered and, at least on the surface, more enlightened and humane than the one ruled by the crude, brutal Cronus.

The Greeks regularly exploited this theme of rebellion against an old order in their own lives. During the three centuries leading up to Athens's creation of the world's first democracy shortly before 500 B.C., there was frequent political experimentation across the Greek lands. Not only in Athens, but in numerous other city-states as well, people became dissatisfied with traditional autocratic systems. In them, either one man or a small group of men, always local aristocrats, or nobles, ruled and made the important decisions for the rest of the citizens.

Hoping to better their lives by bringing about fairer government, groups of ordinary citizens demanded change. In Athens, from which the most detailed evidence for these radical reforms comes, the common people occasionally resorted to violence to effect change. Slowly but surely, such insurrections against the past or status quo made Athens increasingly democratic, and eventually full-blown democracy emerged in that city-state, making history in the process.

In a way, then, the Athenians who rebelled against their older political systems could justify their actions by pointing to the revolt of Zeus and his siblings against the Titans. As part of their reconstruction of the world, Zeus and his companions erected several magnificent palaces atop Greece's highest peak, Mount Olympus. For that reason, they became known as the Olympians. (This was actually a generalization. A few of these gods either rarely visited or eventually left Olympus.)

A common belief exists today that because of this creation myth the Classical Greeks believed that their gods literally and physically dwelled on Olympus's summit. But this was not the case. It is possible that in very early times, perhaps during the Dark Age, some or even many people accepted that notion. But over time it became a mere folk belief. Even in the *Iliad,* composed a bit before the dawn of Classical times, there are hints that Mount Olympus was more of a symbol of the gods, a sort of metaphor for their

Mount Olympus, in northern Greece. In the Dark Age, some or all Greeks thought the gods dwelled there. In the centuries that followed, however, most Greeks held that those deities lived somewhere in the sky.

power, than their real abode. By the advent of the era of Pericles, Plato, and Aristotle, the general assumption was that the gods, if they existed at all, dwelled somewhere in the sky or in a distant place humans could never visit.

Wherever the gods lived, Zeus was their overlord. He took his sister Hera as his wife, and she became the protector of marriage. Zeus's brothers also assumed important roles in the new Olympian order. Poseidon gained the office of lord of the seas and was closely associated with horses and dolphins, which, along with the trident, became his symbols. Meanwhile, Hades took charge of the Underworld, and Zeus's other sisters each played one or more crucial roles in nature and, later, in human affairs. Demeter oversaw agriculture, and Hestia became protector of the hearth, which was the center of every Greek home. In most families, the father or other head of the household began every meal with a prayer and sometimes an offering to her. Another divine sister, Aphrodite, goddess of love, did not have parents per se. She arose from a mass of sea foam that surrounded Uranus's genitals after Cronus had severed them and thrown them into the sea. Her symbols were the dove and the rose. The other Olympians included Ares (the Roman Mars), god of war; Athena (Minerva), goddess of wisdom and war and protector of civilized life; Hermes (Mercury), the messenger god and patron of travelers; Artemis (Diana), who oversaw the moon and the hunt and protected young girls; her twin brother Apollo (Apollo), god of the sun, prophecy, healing, music, and archery; Dionysus (Bacchus), god of the grapevine, wine, and fertility; and Hephaestus (Vulcan), god of the forge and protector of craftspersons, whom Hera had mysteriously conceived on her own, without any union with Zeus.

Men from Mud

At the time that Zeus and his Olympians were building their palaces and restoring the earth's surface, humans did not yet exist. The Greeks had two separate creation myths to explain how people came to be. The first claimed that the gods fashioned several races of humans, all but one of which was more unworthy than the one before it.

Much more popular among the Classical Greeks was the creation story that featured the Titan Prometheus. He was the one who had foreseen that the way to defeat the Titans was to release the monsters from Tartarus. Indeed, he was the wisest of all the gods. It was no wonder that Zeus made him his chief adviser.

In fact, Zeus was so enthralled by Prometheus's wisdom and skills that he assigned him the important task of creating a race of mortals. Eagerly accepting the job, the Titan kneeled down in a patch of mud and began fashioning it into various kinds of figures. At first he was unsure of how a human should look. But then he realized that these mortals were going to have a close relationship with the gods. It only made sense, therefore, that they should *look* like the gods.

After he had created several mud-figures with bodies like his own, Prometheus realized it was time to animate them, or endow them with movement and thought. In

A Roman sarcophagus relief depicts Prometheus, sitting, left, sculpting and creating man from mud as the goddess Athena looks on.

The Forgotten Goddess

One of the deities who lived on Mt. Olympus, Hebe, daughter of Zeus and Hera, was not one of the major Olympian gods. Hebe was the goddess of youth and a cupbearer to the major gods. Except for her marriage to the famous hero Heracles after his death and resurrection, she appeared in no myths.

some accounts, this occurred thanks to some sparks of life left over from when Eros had brought together the countless fragments that had been swirling in Chaos. Other ancient stories claimed that Athena helped the Titan by breathing life into the clay figures.

Not long after Prometheus had created the first people, he watched them from a distance and quickly grew sad. It disturbed him to see how hard they had to struggle just to stay alive. During the winter they nearly froze to death, and they were constantly threatened by wild beasts, which were difficult to kill without metal weapons. Knowledge of fire, Prometheus knew, would allow his creations to stay warm in winter and to melt metals to make proper weapons and tools. The problem was that Zeus had forbidden him to give the humans fire. That gift was reserved only for the immortal gods, the leading Olympian had declared.

Prometheus thought long and hard about what he should do and finally made a fateful decision. Behind Zeus's back, he stole some fire from the gods' hearth and hurriedly took it to the humans. In Rouse's account, the Titan

> began to teach men in earnest. He showed them how to cook, and how to keep themselves warm; how to make bricks and burn pottery; how to melt metals and make tools. Men lived no longer in caves and holes in the earth, but made houses to live in. Prometheus taught them how to write and how to do arithmetic. . . . In fact, he taught them the beginnings of all the arts.[16]

Prometheus's disobedience toward Zeus is another example of rebellion in the Greek myths. Like Zeus's attempt to stop the suffering of his swallowed siblings, Prometheus's revolt against Zeus was intended to halt the suffering of the puny creatures the Titan had recently fashioned. Fire, Prometheus realized, would definitely improve the quality of their lives.

But at this point in time, Zeus did not care about the quality of the humans' lives. It did not take him long to discover that his favorite Titan had violated his trust. Fuming with anger, the king of Olympus decided to make an example of him, so that no other gods would contemplate disobedience. Zeus ordered that Prometheus be chained to a large boulder near the top of a distant mountain. There, each day a huge eagle (or in some accounts a vulture) chewed out the Titan's liver. Later, in the evening, after the bird had left, the organ grew back, and the next day the grisly cycle repeated itself.

The Power of Myths

Every Greek was familiar with this myth about Prometheus's crime and punishment in the same way that most people today know how Luke Skywalker discovered the identity of his real father. It is not surprising, therefore, that an ancient playwright dramatized the Titan's stirring tale. About the year 460 B.C., the Athenian Aeschylus wrote and staged *Prometheus Bound,* which dramatizes Prometheus's moral courage and noble spirit. In the play, after the chained god has suffered for several years, Zeus offers him a deal. He will free him from his torments if he agrees to provide some information about a future event. (Prometheus had been born with the ability to see into the future.) But the Titan refuses. As a matter of principle, he courageously points out that giving fire to humans was the right thing to do and that Zeus's punishment is unjust and cruel. The chief god threatens to inflict new, more terrifying penalties on the impertinent Titan. Yet the valiant Prometheus still refuses to give in.

As Greek audiences watched this extraordinary, moving tragedy unfold, they recognized an important lesson in the story. Like Prometheus, they felt that doing the right thing was important, even if it meant defying authority and paying a heavy price for it—or at least they hoped that if they were ever in such a position they might be as brave and upstanding as he was.

Also, as noted scholar C.M. Bowra points out, when Greeks *did* make such a hard and heroic choice, it was

Prometheus Unbound

The ancient Greeks who watched Aeschylus's grand drama *Prometheus Bound,* about Prometheus's cruel punishment by Zeus, were not likely to have been satisfied with the ending. In it, Zeus forces the heroic Prometheus to spend eternity in torment. It would make sense that playgoers would expect the author to follow up with a sequel in which the hero's courage and goodness would eventually be rewarded. In fact, some evidence does suggest that *Prometheus Bound* was intended as the second play in a trilogy that Aeschylus never finished. The plot of the third play, *Prometheus Unbound,* remains unknown. However, it can be pieced together with some certainty from the popular myths about Prometheus. At the start of the third play, the eagle would still be tearing out the chained god's liver every day. Also, it would be made clear that Prometheus knows full

well that he can end his suffering simply by summoning Zeus and revealing the information the god seeks. Prometheus would remain resolute and refuse to give in to Zeus, however. Toward the end of the play, the bound god would gain his freedom in one of two ways, depending on which myth Aeschylus chose to follow. In one, the kindly centaur (creature half-man and half-horse) Chiron offers to die in Prometheus's place, and Zeus accepts this offer. In an alternate myth, the famous strongman Heracles appears, kills the eagle, and releases Prometheus. Either way, the latter would gain his freedom, at last satisfying Greek audiences.

Aeschylus's drama Prometheus Bound *is still performed today.*

"not for hope of ultimate reward" in heaven. Rather, it was "because their own natures impelled them to do it." To be "good in themselves"—that is, to be good simply because one's conscience and honor demanded it—was "long a feature of Greek thought."[17] Moreover, a major reason that most Greeks felt this way was that their myths contained examples—as in the case of Prometheus—of gods and heroes doing the right thing out of courage and an innate sense of morality.

CHAPTER **3**

The Heroes of Troy and Other Champions

Greek mythology is filled with the exploits of heroes, including those who save their fellow humans by slaying monsters and/or performing seemingly superhuman tasks. They more than match the model for the ancient hero that appears in the mythologies of peoples across the world, from Europe to Asia to the Americas. That universal model of the mythical hero is concisely described by noted classical scholar Michael Grant:

> The hero must use his superior qualities at all times to excel and win applause, for that is the reward and demonstration of his manhood. He makes honor his paramount code, and glory the driving force and aim of his existence. [His] ideals are courage, endurance, strength and beauty. . . . Although he is no god, there is something about him which brings him not too far from heaven.[18]

Thus, by braving incredible dangers, the hero sets an example for average humans in his society. Moreover, his courage and exploits suggest that ordinary people might be capable of doing great things if they would only set larger-than-normal goals and devote the proper time and energy to achieving them. At the same time, a number of these heroes of old had personal flaws or faults such as arrogance, a nasty temper, or blindness to the truth. In listening to their stories unfold, people could learn important lessons about character and personal ethics. On the one hand, they might be inspired by a legendary character's strengths, and on the other they might try to avoid the character's mistakes.

The Trojan War

Of the many heroes in the Greek myths who inspired people and taught them lessons, none were more revered and honored by the Classical Greeks than the intrepid warriors who fought at Troy. Whether or not the legendary Trojan War was a real event, the Greeks believed it was. For them it was a watershed of their civilization, one that set an eternal example of courage, fortitude, patriotism, and reverence for the gods. Therefore, the myths associated with that conflict were seen as more important than any others.

The Greeks collected the ancient sources for those tales into what later came to be called the Trojan Cycle of myths. Chief among said sources were Homer's *Iliad* and *Odyssey*. Other important sources dealing with the events of the Trojan War and its aftermath were six of the works from the Epic Cycle. They included the *Cypria, Aethiopis, Sack of Troy, Little Iliad, Nostoi,* and *Telegony*. Generally, these covered events that Homer had not described in his epics. For example, the *Cypria* covered the events leading up to the war and the conflict's early stages.

Likewise, the *Nostoi* (*Homecomings*) told how the Greek leaders (excluding Odysseus) made it home after their victory.

It was the *Cypria* that described the ultimate cause of the conflict at Troy; namely, the love affair between Helen and Paris. Helen, wife of Menelaus, king of the Greek kingdom of Sparta, was the most beautiful of all mortal women. She was so physically strik-

Uncovering Troy

In the 1800s, German businessman Heinrich Schliemann became fascinated with Homer's *Iliad*. At the time, experts thought the Trojan War was a tall tale. But Schliemann believed it was real. So he set out to find Troy and succeeded. In 1871 he began excavating at a mound in western Turkey and found Troy's ruins.

ing that at one time or another all the Greek kings had expressed their love for her. Once she had chosen Menelaus to be her husband, her father had made the other royal suitors swear they would aid Menelaus if another man broke up their marriage.

Paris was a prince of Troy, a city-state that lay on the far side of the blue Aegean Sea. He had heard about Helen's incomparable beauty and went to Sparta to see her for himself. With the aid of Aphrodite, goddess of love, he was welcomed as a guest in Menelaus's palace in Sparta. Soon after Paris's arrival, Menelaus departed on a business trip to Crete. In the weeks that followed, Paris and Helen fell in love and the young man persuaded her to leave her husband and go home with him to Troy.

Upon returning to Sparta, Menelaus was shocked and enraged to hear that his wife had betrayed him and run away with Paris. Wasting no time, the Spartan king went to Mycenae, northeast of Sparta, where his brother Agamemnon was

The Cypria *describes Helen of Sparta fleeing with her lover, Paris of Troy. This event started the Trojan War.*

king. Agamemnon offered to enlist the aid of the other Greek kings, who had earlier given their oaths to help Menelaus if someone broke up his marriage. Each of these rulers gathered a contingent of ships and troops and joined Agamemnon, who assumed command of the large-scale expedition against the Trojans.

Not long afterward, the great war fleet reached Troy. When the Greeks went ashore, they saw that the city was fronted by a wide, windy plain, a perfect place for soldiers and siege devices to approach its walls. Those walls, however, were very tall and well fortified, but the Greeks were confident of victory because among their number were many skilled, heroic warriors. One of the greatest was Ajax, who was known for his massive physical frame and enormous strength. Another was Odysseus, ruler of the island kingdom of Ithaca, renowned for his cleverness. Greatest of all the Greek warriors who went to Troy was Achilles, son of the divine nymph Thetis and a mortal king named Peleus. Almost from the beginning of his life, Achilles and his mother knew he was destined for greatness, especially as a warrior.

When the Greeks landed near Troy they found a well fortified city with massive walls on the hill of Hisarlik. The siege of Troy would last ten years.

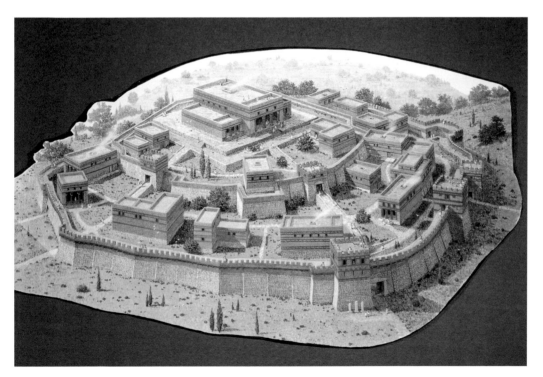

When he was a baby, she had dipped his body in the Styx, the river separating the Underworld from the realm of mortals. This had made him invulnerable to injury—only the heel by which she had held him when dipping him in the river was not protected. A supremely confident individual, he recognized and reveled in his own importance and believed it would be better to have a short life leading to eternal glory rather than a long one that would never be remembered.

Characters of Eternal Renown

For the Classical Greeks, Achilles was the utmost example of a person with *arete* (ahr-uh-TAY), a combination of moral excellence and warlike valor. So influential was he in Greek society that some men strove for fame and glory in the same way he did. The most famous example was Macedonia's Alexander III, later called "Alexander the Great," who conquered much of the Middle East in the fourth century B.C. It is said that he slept with a copy of the *Iliad* under his pillow and thought he was a new-day Achilles. Alexander, too, believed he was fated to have a short but glorious life and at one point told his men, "Those who endure hardship and danger are the ones who achieve glory, and the most gratifying thing is to live with courage and to die leaving behind eternal renown."[19]

The Classical Greeks were no less moved and inspired by a number of other heroes who appeared to be role models for qualities such as honor, bravery, and selflessness. Theseus's willingness to go to Crete and face the ferocious Minotaur in order to save his fellow citizens was an example. So was Perseus's courageous search for and confrontation with the horrifying Medusa.

Especially inspiring to many Greeks was the famous strongman Heracles (whom the Romans later called Hercules, the name by which he is better known today). Heracles was known for his big-heartedness, his courage, and his phenomenal strength. That last quality was not surprising because he was a son of the leader of the gods, Zeus, who had produced him through mating with a mortal woman named Alcmena. Some of Zeus's superhuman strength had been passed on to the intrepid Heracles.

This wine jug from 550–530 B.C. depicts Heracles slaying the Nemean lion, one of his twelve labors.

Dozens of myths featured Heracles and his exploits, including the famous twelve labors, in which the strongman performed a series of tasks that were beyond the abilities of ordinary people. They included breaking the neck of a rampaging lion with his bare hands, capturing a savage giant bull, and rounding up and taming a herd of terrifying man-eating horses. The feat that more than any other showed Heracles's great courage and honor, however, was when he faced the god of death, Thanatos.

This great confrontation between Heracles and Thanatos takes place in the myth of Alcestis, wife of Admetus, king of the Pherae, in central Greece. Unbeknownst to the strongman, Admetus is dying and Alcestis has offered to take her husband's place when Thanatos comes to seize him and take him to the Underworld. Heracles, who is on his way to perform one of his twelve labors, arrives in Pherae shortly before Thanatos's appearance and learns what is about to happen. The sympathetic and honorable Heracles takes it upon himself to stop Thanatos from taking either Alcestis or Admetus. In the words of the Athenian playwright Euripides, who dramatized the myth for the stage, Heracles declares:

> The woman's dead; and I must rescue her. . . . The black-robed king of the dead will come to drink the blood of victims offered at her tomb. That's where I'll find him. I'll hide there, watch for him, leap out and spring on him; and once I have my arms locked round his bruised ribs, there's no power on earth that will be able to wrench him free, till he gives her up to me![20]

Heracles keeps his vow. When the god of death arrives, the strongman jumps out, seizes the dark figure, and fights him with all his might. Being a god, Thanatos is extremely strong, of course. But having the blood of Zeus in his veins, Heracles proves stronger and defeats his ghastly opponent. Realizing he has been foiled, Thanatos leaves, thereby allowing both Admetus and Alcestis to live long lives together.

Men of Honor and Courage

Courage and honor similar to that displayed by Heracles is a frequent theme in the myths about the Trojan War, and whereas many of the participants in these stories perform heroic deeds, none were more inspiring than Achilles and his chief opponent, Hector, son of Priam, king of Troy. Their classic confrontation occurs in the tenth year of the war. Achilles has had a quarrel with the leader of the Greek expedition, Agamemnon, and in his anger refuses to come out of his tent and fight. As a result, many of the Greek fighters lose heart, and the Trojans begin to gain the advantage. In a flash of his own considerable valor, Patroclus, Achilles's best friend, borrows Achilles's armor and goes into battle, hoping

The Excellent All-Rounder

The late noted scholar H.D.F. Kitto gave this explanation for arete, *an ancient Greek word that is difficult to translate precisely into English.*

If *arete* is used in a general context, [it] will connote [indicate] excellence in the ways in which a man can be excellent—morally, intellectually, physically, practically. Thus, the hero of the *Odyssey* is a great fighter, a wily schemer, a ready speaker, a man of stout heart and broad wisdom who knows that he must endure without too much complaining what the gods send. And he can both build and sail a boat . . . beat a young braggart at throwing the discus, challenge [men] at boxing, wrestling, or running, [and] be moved to tears by a song. He is in fact the excellent all-rounder. He has surpassing *arete*. So, too, does the hero of the older poem [the *Iliad*], Achilles—the most formidable of fighters, the swiftest of runners, and the noblest of soul. . . . The Greek hero tried to combine in himself the virtues which our own heroic age [medieval times] divided between the knight and the churchman.

H.D.F. Kitto. *The Greeks*. Piscataway, NJ: Aldine Transaction, 2007, p. 172.

the Trojans will retreat because they think Achilles has reentered the fray. But Hector engages Patroclus and slays him.

When Achilles hears that his friend is dead, he immediately patches up his differences with Agamemnon and throws himself back into the battle. Elated, the other Greeks again take heart and follow him in a mighty offensive that drives the Trojans all the way back to their city walls. Desperate to reach safety, they hurriedly stream through the gates and slam them shut.

Only valiant Hector stays outside, alone on the windy plain, clearly waiting for Achilles. He does not have to wait long. Achilles soon approaches out of the Greek ranks, in Homer's words, "looking like the god of war in his flashing helmet."[21] The two greatest warriors in the known world now clash in a stirring battle for the ages, an awe-inspiring duel that has the crowds on both sides cheering. Finally, Achilles manages to get the advantage and drives his spear into Hector's throat. Hector topples into the dirt, and the light of life fades from his eyes. Within seconds, as Homer writes, "his disembodied soul took wing for the House of Hades."[22]

The Classical Greeks knew the tale of Achilles and Hector well. In fact, many young Greek men memorized large sections of the *Iliad* while studying it in school. In addition, parents told their children the story, along with others about brave, honorable, mythical characters, and story-tellers recited the Homeric epics in public gatherings. All Greeks could relate to Achilles's honor in avenging his friend Patroclus's death at Hector's hands. They could also admire Hector's honor, courage, and selflessness in defending his homeland by staying and facing the greatest of the Greek warriors in single combat. The Greek city-states and kingdoms often warred among themselves. So ordinary people—mostly farmers and shopkeepers—had to sometimes don armor and go out and fight for the honor and preservation of their homelands. As they approached the enemy lines, many realized that they had been thrust into circumstances similar to those experienced by the Homeric heroes. It was therefore expected of them to give their all, like those heroes had done.

Reverse Role Models

The Greeks were well aware that some of these same heroes they sought to emulate on the battlefield had personal faults that should *not* be copied.

With all of his courage and fighting skills, Achilles, for example, was very vain and arrogant, as seen in his driving, unquenchable desire for eternal fame. He was willing to die young as long as his deeds would be remembered for all time. This was exactly what happened, as a poisoned Trojan arrow struck him down (hitting him in his vulnerable heel) not long after he had slain Hector.

Achilles Against Hector

One of most popular translations of Homer's Iliad *in the twentieth century was the one by the distinguished scholar W.H.D. Rouse. This passage from Rouse's version describes the climactic confrontation between Achilles and Hector.*

Achilles moved to meet him full of fury, covering his chest with the resplendent [dazzling] shield [and holding] the great spear, which gleamed like the finest of all the stars of heaven. . . . He scanned Hector with ruthless heart, to see where the white flesh gave the best opening for a blow. Hector was well-covered with that splendid armor which he had stripped from Patroclus, but an opening showed where the collar-bones join the neck to the shoulder, the gullet, where a blow brings quickest death. There Achilles aimed, and the point went through the soft neck. [Hector] fell in the dust, and Achilles cried in triumph, [saying] "I have brought you low! Now you shall be mauled by vultures and dogs!"

Homer. *Iliad*. Translated by W.H.D. Rouse. New York: Signet, 2007, p. 261.

After slaying Hector, Achilles dragged his corpse behind his chariot three times around the walls of Troy as the Trojans lamented.

The Greeks sometimes witnessed real-life examples of Achilles's extreme conceit and tendency toward overachievement. In the fourth century B.C. Alexander the Great identified himself with Achilles, followed his lead, and sought everlasting renown. But most Greeks did not want to be like Alexander, whose obsession with power and glory led to his untimely death in his early thirties. So, in a way, Achilles could also be a reverse role model, an example of what might happen when someone pursued excessive goals and overindulged in certain behaviors.

The great Heracles himself could also at times be a reverse role model. His tragic flaw was an excessively violent temper, which got him into trouble on more than one occasion. The worst example was when he fell into a fit of rage and killed his wife and children. After recovering his wits and realizing what he had done, he wanted to commit suicide. But his close friend, the hero Theseus, arrived in the nick of time and stopped him. Theseus convinced Heracles to choose life, in part because the world would be worse off without a hero of his stature.

A fifth-century B.C. red figure crater depicts Jason bringing Pelias of Iolcos the Golden Fleece.

Another mythical hero who possessed serious flaws was Jason, a royal prince who hailed from Iolcos, in east-central Greece. He at first accomplished admirable deeds and displayed a sense of honor, but later in life he revealed a dark side and ended up destroying his good reputation. When very young, Jason learned that his father's throne had been stolen by a relative named Pelias. When he was old enough to challenge Pelias, Jason arrived at the palace and demanded justice. But the usurper said that the young man must first prove he was worthy of being king: If Jason could find and bring back the Golden Fleece—the magical skin of a fabulous ram—Pelias would gladly give up the throne.

Pelias was lying, of course. He expected Jason to die while trying to find the fleece. But the stalwart and brave Jason confounded this plan by mounting an expedition manned by several heroes, including Heracles, and finding the fleece in the faraway land of Colchis, on the northern shore of the Black Sea. With the aid of a local princess, Medea, who had fallen in love with him, Jason retrieved the fleece and brought it back to Iolcos.

To Jason's surprise Pelias refused to fulfill his earlier promise to hand over the throne. The dispute between the two men dragged on for a few years, during which time Jason and Medea had two children together. Eventually, the angry Jason began acting in ways unbefitting a hero. Perhaps at his urging, Medea, who was a sorceress, convinced the king's three daughters to kill their father and cut him into pieces. Before Jason could grab the throne, however, Pelias's son Acastus branded both Jason and Medea murderers and drove them and their young children from the city. After that, Jason turned on his wife, rejected her, and married a princess from another city. To punish Jason for this betrayal, the gods abandoned him, and he died alone and unhappy. (Meanwhile, Medea got her own revenge on Jason by killing their children.)

Odysseus's Wanderings

At least the ill effects of Heracles's and Jason's crimes were confined to themselves and their immediate families. Sometimes in the Greek myths the character flaw of a hero causes him to commit a crime that negatively affects the lives of hundreds of other people, many of them strangers. Just such an incident occurred in the last stage of the Trojan War.

The Greeks eventually won the conflict and destroyed and looted Troy. During this rampage, the notable warrior-hero Ajax the Lesser broke into the local temple of Athena. This unworthy act was inspired in part by the man's anger and hurt pride over an earlier episode in which the goddess had made him lose a footrace so that a contestant she favored would win. So the bitter Ajax entered Athena's private abode and dragged away a Trojan princess who was praying there.

Hearing what Ajax had done, Athena determined to punish not only him but also many of his fellow Greek soldiers who had fought at Troy. She persuaded the sea god Poseidon to whip up a huge storm. The tempest engulfed the Greek fleets as they were sailing homeward from Troy and many of those aboard the vessels were killed.

The Greeks who probably suffered most for Ajax's anger and unwise behavior were Odysseus, king of Ithaca, and his men. Odysseus had been the one who had devised a clever way to bring about the Trojans' defeat. Following his instructions, a gang of Greek soldiers had built a huge, hollow, wooden horse that "stood high as a mountain," in Homer's words. Then they "secretly hid selected troops inside its dark void, till its whole huge cavernous belly was stuffed with men at arms," one of whom was Odysseus. Meanwhile, the Greek fleet sailed away until they were out of sight of Troy "and hid their ships on a desolate shore."[23]

The next day the Trojans looked out at the beach and to their surprise and relief saw that the Greek fleet was gone. Thinking the massive horse was a gift left for the gods, they dragged it inside the city and celebrated into the night until everyone, save for a few sentries, was fast asleep. At that point, Odysseus and his men crawled from their hiding place inside the horse. They silently slew

A Faux Horse

The wooden horse built for the 1956 movie *Helen of Troy*, about the Trojan War, was made of balsa wood and the extras who dragged it into the city had to pretend that it was heavy.

Greek soldiers climb from the belly of the Trojan Horse to begin the sack of Troy. Odysseus came up with the idea of the Trojan Horse.

the sentries and opened the gates for the Greek army, which had quietly returned in the dark of night. An orgy of destruction followed, as the Greeks sacked proud Priam's city.

After Troy's fall, Odysseus and his men boarded their twelve ships and sailed for Ithaca. But the storm Poseidon had unleashed at Athena's request caused them to lose their way so badly that they were forced to wander from one exotic and dangerous place to another for years.

One of the places they happened on was an island inhabited by a race of one-eyed giants, the Cyclopes. Odysseus and twelve of his men went ashore to search for food but soon found themselves trapped in the cave of a Cyclops named Polyphemus, who suddenly seized two of them. Odysseus later recounted how the Cyclops "dashed their heads against the floor as though they had been puppies. Their brains ran out on the ground and soaked the earth. Limb by limb, he tore them to pieces to make his meal. We could do nothing but weep and lift up our hands to Zeus."[24]

The hideous giant killed several more of the Greeks before Odysseus finally outwitted him, and he and his remaining men escaped. After numerous other hair-raising adventures, during which the rest of his men met their deaths, Odysseus finally made it home.

The Classical Greeks who read about his wanderings in Homer's *Odyssey* knew that Odysseus had not deserved to pay such a high price for the sins of another. There was a serious double lesson to be learned here. First, one person's failings or crimes have the potential to affect the fate of one's neighbors, and perhaps one's whole community. Therefore it was important to avoid rash or criminal behavior that might hurt one's fellow citizens. Second, one must not commit sacrilege of any kind against the gods, who might well retaliate by punishing innocent people along with the guilty parties.

The Trojan Ram

Did the famous Trojan Horse actually exist? Some modern researchers think it did in a way. They suggest the horse in the myth is an imprecise memory of a large battering ram. It was common in the ancient Middle East, they point out, to make the front of such a siege device look like a horse's head.

Men Who Gave Their Lives

Like Jason, Heracles, Achilles, and other Bronze Age heroes, Odysseus was a mythical person; however, when these characters were on their best behavior they regularly inspired heroic behavior in real Greek men during Classical times. The most noteworthy and noble way those men emulated the heroes was to give their lives in defense of their homes, families, and way of life.

This was what several Athenian soldiers did in the winter of 431–430 B.C. It was during the first year of a terrible war, and Athens's leading general, Pericles, honored the fallen

Blinding a Giant

The incident in which Odysseus and his men blind the Cyclops Polyphemus is one of the most famous in Homer's *Odyssey*. In summary, after the Greeks were trapped in the giant's cave, he killed and ate four of them. The next morning, Polyphemus left to graze his livestock. When he returned that evening, he made still another meal of two men and then guzzled down a great deal of wine. Next, he demanded to know the Greek leader's name. To this query, Odysseus shrewdly answered that his name was "Nobody." Later, the Cyclops fell asleep, and Odysseus and his remaining men sharpened a wooden beam and heated it in the fire. Then they lifted it, Odysseus recalled (in Homer's words),

> and rammed it deep in his crater eye, and I leaned on it, turning it as a shipwright turns a drill. . . . So with our [fire]brand we bored that great eye socket while blood ran out around the red hot bar. Eyelid and lash were seared. The pierced [eye]ball hissed broiling, and the roots popped. . . . The Cyclops bellowed and the rocks roared round him. . . . Clawing his face he tugged the bloody spike out of his eye [and] then he set up a howl for the Cyclopes who lived in caves on windy peaks nearby.

But when the other giants appeared outside the cave and asked who was hurting him, Polyphemus remembered the name Odysseus had given him and told them that Nobody was hurting him! Hearing this, the other Cyclopes figured he had had too much to drink and went home. The next day, the crafty Odysseus and his men made good their escape.

Homer. *Odyssey*. Translated by Robert Fitzgerald. Garden City, NY: Doubleday, 1963, pp. 156-157.

Odysseus outwits, then blinds the Cyclops Polyphemus and escapes being eaten. Some of his men were not so lucky.

with a moving funeral oration. His now-famous words captured the recurring Greek ideal of heroes receiving eternal glory, a concept forged in ancient myths like those of Achilles and Heracles. "You should fix your eyes every day on the greatness of Athens," Pericles proclaimed. "Then reflect that what made her great was men [like these]. They gave her their lives, to her and to all of us [and] won praises that never grow old. [Indeed] their glory remains eternal in men's minds."[25]

CHAPTER 4

The Will of the Gods

T he world of the ancient Greek myths was, as was the real Greek world, one in which people often paid the consequences of their crimes, sins, and other transgressions. In everyday Greek life, the individuals who decided what such consequences would be and meted out the punishments varied from one Greek state to another. In general, there were no police officers, as there are in modern societies, nor were there any lawyers to represent someone in court. So in many places the custom was for the victim of a crime to accuse the perpetrator in public and prosecute him or her in a court. The accused defended him- or herself in the proceeding. For particularly heinous crimes, like treason, a ruler, ruling council, or assembly of the people might call for the accused person's arrest and oversee the trial.

Often, however, ancient Greek societies allowed what might be called natural forces to deal with matters of crime and punishment. It was not unusual, for instance, for the family members of someone who was raped or killed to take the law into their own hands and hunt down and punish the guilty party themselves. This was called taking vengeance.

Similarly, many people believed that criminals, no matter how they were handled by human society, would eventually pay the ultimate price—divine judgment. Indeed, most

Greeks believed that the ultimate judges of right and wrong, as well as the ultimate punishers of the wicked, were the gods. A family that took vengeance could justify its actions by saying that it was carrying out the will of the gods. Also, when someone accused of wrongdoing later died in an accident or of disease or other natural causes, most people in the community were sure, or at least suspected, that the death was caused by divine intervention.

As a result of such beliefs, many Greeks feared the wrath of the gods. This made acts such as publicly denouncing these deities and crimes like robbing temples and defacing cult images of the gods fairly rare. People knew the will of the gods in these matters, along with what might happen to those who committed such unwise acts, because of myths. Most of these stories depicted the divinities doing one of two things. They either protected and rewarded those who followed and upheld the divine will, or they punished the impious—those who went against the will of the gods.

Divine Protection

The Greeks believed that one way a god protected a community of god-fearing people was to become the divine patron of that community. Each city-state in the Classical Age had a patron deity who was thought to watch over its residents. In C.M. Bowra's words, "a whole people might feel that it was protected by watchful presences and united in its admiration for them and its sense of belonging to them."[26] The patron deity of Athens was its namesake, Athena. The Athenians cited a popular myth that explained how she had long ago assumed this protective role. In this tale, she and the sea god Poseidon had taken part in a contest to decide which of them would become Athens's patron. Whichever deity performed the most spectacular feat, as decided by Zeus and some other divine judges, would be the winner. Poseidon touched the Acropolis, the highest point in the city, with his trident, producing a miraculous saltwater spring. The judges thought this was quite impressive. But then Athena made an olive tree grow atop the dry, rocky hill, an accomplishment that caused the judges to declare her the victor.

The Erechtheum on the Acropolis was built to house the olive-wood statue of the goddess Athena. Its construction illustrates the bond between the patron deity and her chosen community.

Another myth both solidified the protective relationship between Athena and the community and taught the Greeks how some important rituals of worship connected to her had originated. In this tale, the goddess hurled down from the sky an olive-wood statue of herself. It landed on the Acropolis's northern edge, and on that spot the Athenians built a temple called the Erechtheum. Resting within that structure in Classical times was a sacred statue that tradition said was the very one that Athena had thrown down to earth in the dim past.

The construction of the Erechtheum illustrated a crucial aspect of the bond between a patron deity and his or her chosen community. To be better able to watch over and protect the residents, the god needed a local house or shelter to stay in when visiting the community. Each Greek state therefore erected at least one and sometimes several temples dedicated to its patron. In addition to the Erechtheum, the Athenians built other temples to Athena, including the magnificent Parthenon, which modern architects often call the most perfect structure ever created. Because Athena was thought actually to reside in her temples from time to time, it was vital to respect her privacy. So no major worship took place inside the building. Instead, sacrifices and other rituals took place at altars set up on the temple's steps or on other parts of its grounds.

Another way that myths showed the Greeks that the gods would protect pious people was by recalling specific incidents in which a god or goddess had rewarded or helped someone. One of the most popular legendary tales of this kind was the charming story of Baucis and Philemon. It tells how one of Zeus's favorite diversions was to disguise himself as a human and travel through villages and towns to see what people were up to. One day he and his messenger, Hermes, donned beggars' outfits and visited a certain Greek region to test the hospitality of the locals. The two gods were dismayed to find that selfishness and cruelty were widespread. Every time they knocked on someone's door and humbly asked for a scrap of food, that person rudely told them to go away.

Zeus and Hermes were about to give up on the inhabitants of that land when they arrived at the smallest, poorest hovel they had yet seen. This time when they knocked on the door, an elderly husband and wife named Baucis and Philemon warmly welcomed them. According to Ovid's version of the story, "They had grown old together in the same cottage. They were very poor, but faced their poverty with [a] cheerful spirit and made its burden light by not complaining."[27] The smiling couple made the strangers comfortable. Then they prepared them a meal of radishes, cabbage, eggs, olives, and other edible tidbits they had gathered.

After the four had consumed their humble meal, Zeus and Hermes revealed themselves to Baucis and Philemon. They thanked them for their hospitality,

A Dangerous Mind

Among the occasional Greeks prosecuted for impiety—either disrespecting or denying the gods' existence—was the famous philosopher Socrates. Although the charge was untrue, the Athenians executed Socrates in 399 B.C. One of his followers, Plato, later movingly described his mentor's death.

took them to a nearby mountaintop, and ordered them to stay there for a while. Zeus then proceeded to flood the region, causing all of the rude folks he had encountered to drown. Afterward, only the old couple's tiny hut remained standing. Zeus transformed this crude dwelling into a beautiful temple with a large, comfortable house beside it. Thereafter, Baucis

Zeus's Flood a Real Event?

The flood sent by Zeus to destroy a region of the Greek world, as recounted in the myth of Baucis and Philemon, was one of several references in Greek mythology to floods divinely inflicted on humans for various misdeeds. A number of modern scholars think that these legendary depictions of floods, in some cases including towering sea waves (tsunamis), may have been loosely based on a real natural disaster. In about 1620 B.C., at the start of the late Bronze Age, the volcano on the small island of Thera (now called Santorini), located just north of Crete, erupted with unprecedented violence. At the height of the event, Thera's entire central section collapsed into the sea and huge tsunamis spread outward in all directions.

Some hammered the Minoan settlements located near the coasts of Crete. Others plowed into the shores of the Greek mainland. It is possible that oral accounts of this catastrophe were passed along over time and became part of the fabric of the Greek myths.

Baucis and Philemon entertain guests who happen to be the gods Zeus and Hermes. Although poor, the couple fed the gods and were spared when Zeus caused the flooding of their town. Zeus made a lavish palace out of their house and the couple became Zeus's devoted priests.

and Philemon lived in the house and tended to the temple as Zeus's devoted priests.

This and some other simple myths demonstrated more than that the gods rewarded those who were religiously devout. Such tales also taught the Classical Greeks that Zeus and the other gods expected humans to observe some basic rules of hospitality. Accordingly, the Greeks developed just such a set of rules, called *xenia,* or "two-way hospitality." In each city-state, each of a number of homes kept a small room vacant and regularly welcomed visitors from other cities to stay there. In return, these hosts knew they would have a place to stay when they visited their guests' home cities. Also, a tradition developed in which hosts served their guests supper on their first night in town, and when it was time for the guests to depart, they and their hosts exchanged small gifts.

Traits the Gods Could Not Abide

Just as a number of myths explained how the gods became protectors of communities and rewarded humans for pious behavior, other stories showed the kinds of behaviors the gods despised. Most of these same myths depicted those deities punishing people for various misbehaviors, sins, and crimes. Among the character traits and behaviors the gods viewed as most distasteful and harmful was greed. They knew that greedy people often became so obsessed with fulfilling their personal desires that they neglected worshipping the gods in the proper manner.

One of the better-known Greek myths dealing with greed and its consequences is humorous on the surface but makes a serious point about civility and right versus wrong conduct. It is the famous tale of King Midas, who ruled part of Anatolia (now Turkey), where a number of Greek cities grew up. He was known for his greed and his desire for fine foods, expensive clothes, furniture, and jewelry. But he especially had a love for gold. On one occasion, Midas encountered Dionysus, the god of fertility and wine. The king had recently done that deity a favor, so Dionysus promised to grant him anything he wished for. Midas immediately requested the ability to turn anything he touched into gold, and the god kept his promise and made it so.

At first Midas had visions of extreme wealth and happiness. But it did not take long for him to realize that he had made a terrible mistake. He was ecstatic when he turned chairs, pillars, rocks, and other objects into gold just by touching them; however, when he sat down to eat his dinner, he was shocked when his food also turned into gold at his mere touch. Soon he was hungrier than he had ever been before and realized he was going to starve to death. Worse still, when his little daughter ran to hug him good morning, she was turned to gold as well. In desperation, Midas prayed to Dionysus and pleaded with him to take away his gift. The god, who had known all along what would happen to Midas, saw that he had learned his lesson and so answered his prayer. Thereafter, a person who was able to make a lot of money was said to have the "Midas touch."

Dionysus gave King Midas the power to turn anything he touched to gold. Midas asked the god to take away his ability after his food and daughter were turned to gold by his touch.

Midas learned his lesson in a fairly painless way and did not suffer any overt punishment, but many other mortals who got on the gods' wrong side were not so fortunate. Another distasteful character trait these deities could not abide in humans was extreme pride or conceit. Such arrogance was seen as particularly unsavory when it was directed against the gods. This is exactly what happened in the case of Arachne, a young Greek woman who became famous for her skill in the arts of weaving, sewing, and embroidery. Every garment she produced seemed fit for a goddess, and people far and wide offered to pay her handsomely if she would make clothes for them.

Unfortunately for Arachne, her personality and good judgment did not match her talents as a seamstress. One day someone remarked that her skills were so great that it seemed as if she had studied under the goddess Athena, divine overseer of craftwork. Arachne arrogantly replied that she needed no goddess to instruct her and that she could easily make better clothes than Athena could. When the goddess heard about these prideful comments, she was insulted. She disguised herself as a feeble old woman and paid Arachne a visit. The concealed goddess said she was aware of the young woman's disparaging remarks about Athena and advised her to apologize for showing such disrespect. But, so Ovid tells it, Arachne arrogantly answered,

> "You come here feeble in mind and worn out with old age, [and] you have lived too long. Let your [daughter], if you have one, listen to you. I have wisdom enough to take care of myself. Why doesn't the goddess come herself? Why does she avoid a contest?" Then the goddess declared, "She has come!" And she threw off the disguise and revealed herself.[28]

Unafraid and conceited as ever, the girl challenged Athena to a weaving contest. The fuming goddess agreed, certain she could outdo the impudent young mortal. But after hours of working at competing looms, Arachne's cloth was every bit as beautiful as Athena's. This was the proverbial last straw for the angry deity, who broke the girl's loom, hit her over the head with a piece of it, and turned her into a spider. Thus it was believed that this is why spiders spin webs. In addition, Arachne's transformation into a spider in the myth motivated modern scientists to call spiders and their relatives *arachnids*.

The Price of Disobedience

Although Athena and her fellow divine beings heartily disapproved of greed and arrogance, some things were worse in their eyes. Among these was disobeying the gods. Thanks to several popular myths, all Greeks knew well that few human transgressions were worse than failing to follow orders given or rules set down by these divinities.

The price for disobeying the gods was almost always high, as the sad story of Orpheus and Eurydice well illustrated. The son of Apollo, the god of music and poetry, and of Calliope (kuh-LY-uh-pee), muse of epic poetry, Orpheus was blessed with an astounding musical talent. The young man was such a great musician that when he played his harp, people, animals, and even plants were deeply moved.

Orpheus eventually met, fell in love with, and married Eurydice (yur-ID-uh-see), a beautiful nymph (minor nature goddess). They enjoyed an exceptionally happy life until one day, without warning, she was bitten by a poisonous snake and died. Devastated, Orpheus boldly descended into the dark reaches of the Underworld to get her back. There, he played his harp for the lord of that grim realm, Hades, who was so impressed that he agreed to let Eurydice return to the world of the living.

There was one condition, however. Orpheus must walk ahead of his wife and never look back at her until they had reached the surface. If the man disobeyed this divine demand, Hades warned, there would be dire consequences that he would regret for the rest of his days. Orpheus carefully followed the god's orders during nearly the entire upward journey. But at the

To Honor Athena

Inside Greek temples erected to honor various gods stood cult images, or statues, of these deities. Some were very large and splendidly decorated. The giant statue of Athena in the Parthenon stood more than 40 feet (12m) high and was made of wood covered in ivory and hundreds of pounds of pure gold.

last moment, he could no longer resist the temptation to look back, and when he did, Eurydice was violently yanked back into the depths, never to return.

Not wanting to suffer a fate like that of Orpheus, many Greeks made sure they kept any promises they had made to the gods during prayer or other worship. People were especially careful about fulfilling oaths they had made to the chief god, Zeus. This was partly because he was the most powerful deity and also because he controlled lightning, storms, and many other natural phenomena. If angry enough, he might unleash these forces on a larger-than-normal scale, causing widespread destruction.

But more than any other reason for obeying Zeus and staying on his good side was the well-known fact that he had never cared very much for humans in the first place. Indeed, if he had had his way in the dim past, the Classical Greeks

Orpheus leads his wife, Eurydice, out of the Underworld. After he had impressed Hades with his harp playing, the god let him and Eurydice return to the living. He was told not to look back before leaving the Underworld, but he did, and Eurydice was brought back to the Underworld never to emerge again.

An Extremely Dysfunctional Family

Among the myths about the curse of the House of Atreus was the tragic tale of King Agamemnon, who commanded the Greek expedition to Troy. When he returned home from the war after ten years, his wife, Clytemnestra, had him killed. As the curse continued, her own son slew her to avenge his father's murder.

would still be living in caves, wearing animal skins, and eating raw meat. After all, Zeus had ordered Prometheus not to give humans knowledge of fire and had severely punished the Titan when he had disobeyed this order. If Zeus was so quick to punish one of his fellow gods for disobedience, the later Greeks reasoned, what might the leader of the gods do to mere mortals who failed to follow his dictates?

In fact, it was a common belief among the Greeks that the human race had already suffered greatly because of Zeus's overzealous punishment of Prometheus. True, thanks to the Titan who had created them, people had permanently gained the gift of fire, which had allowed them to cook their food, extract metals from rocks, and light their homes at night. But as shown in one of the most famous of all the Greek myths, Zeus's desire for vengeance had extended beyond Prometheus's penalty and ensured that humanity would remember the chief god's wrath for all time.

The myth referred to is that of Pandora, whose name means "all gifts." The name derived from the fact that each of several different gods had contributed a specific gift to the process of her creation. As Hesiod tells it in his long poem *Works and Days,* while preparing to punish Prometheus for disobedience, Zeus noticed that all of the humans the Titan had created were male. So the master of Olympus hatched a plan to fashion a second gender, one that would bring humanity a great deal of trouble and grief. Hesiod says that Zeus

> told Hephaestos [god of the forge] quickly to mix earth with water and to put in it a voice and human power to move, to make a face like an immortal goddess, and to shape the lovely figure of a virgin girl. Athena was to teach the girl to weave, and golden Aphrodite to pour charm upon her head. . . . Zeus [also] ordered [Hermes] to [give her] sly manners. . . .[29]

Once the gods had finished shaping Pandora, Hermes guided her down to earth and urged Epimetheus, Prometheus's slow-witted brother, to take her in. Prometheus had earlier told Epimetheus never to accept any gifts from Zeus, but Epimetheus forgot that warning and welcomed Pandora into his home as his wife. She was carrying a large, sealed jar that Zeus had given her. When Epimetheus asked what was in the jar, she replied, quite honestly, that she had no idea. It did not take long for her curiosity to be piqued, however, and, with Epimetheus's aid, she opened the jar. Almost instantaneously, a swirling torrent of evils poured out, among them worries, hate, disease, and all the other problems that still plague humanity today. In this way, Zeus managed to punish the human race for Prometheus's audacious crime of disobedience. Generations after Hesiod's death, his warning echoed through Greek society: "There is no way to escape the will of Zeus."[30]

Pandora holds the jar that she will open and unleash all the world's evils on mankind.

A Despicable Crime

As much as the gods hated for humans to neglect worshipping them or to disobey them, no act violated the will of these deities more than the despicable crime committed by Tantalus, one of Zeus's many half-mortal sons. At first, the gods liked Tantalus so much that they allowed him to dine with them on Mount Olympus. For reasons that no one has ever discovered, however, the man betrayed the deities' trust in a truly repulsive manner. First, he slew his own son, Pelops, and boiled the body in a large pot. Afterward, Tantalus cut up the remains into hundreds of pieces and secretly added them to a stew that was about to be served to the Olympian gods. It was apparently Tantalus's intention to secretly turn the divine beings into lowly, uncivilized cannibals.

But Tantalus's assumption that he could fool the gods so easily was misguided. When they smelled the food he had

placed before them, they immediately knew what was in it. Seething with anger, they jumped to their feet, seized Tantalus, and shackled him so he could not get away. Simply killing him was not a harsh enough punishment for what he had done, they decided, so they threw him down into the Underworld's dark depths. There, many years later, a Greek king who managed to peer into those depths, saw Tantalus's horrendous, eternal suffering and reported that the man was forced to stand

> in a lake up to his chin, always thirsty, but try as he could, not a drop could he lap up. For as often as the poor old man dipped his head to take a drink, the water was sucked back and disappeared. . . . Tall trees in full leaf dangled their fruit over his head, pears and pomegranates, and fine juicy apples, sweet figs and ripe olives. But as often as the poor old man reached out a hand to catch one, the wind tossed them [out of reach].[31]

Fortunately for Pelops, the gods had the power to restore him to life, which they did. There was one problem, however. One of the deities had accidentally consumed a small morsel of the awful meal, so when they put Pelops back together, one of his shoulders was missing. The gods rectified this situation by molding him a new shoulder out of ivory.

Meanwhile, the gods never got over the crime Tantalus had committed against them, and it did not satisfy them merely to punish him alone. So, with the exception of innocent Pelops, they placed a curse on Tantalus's family that lasted for many generations. Because of this "curse of the House of Atreus" (named for Tantalus's grandson, Atreus, whose generation was the first to suffer its consequences), members of the family repeatedly committed horrible acts

---

The gods punished Tantalus for dismembering his son by having him stand for eternity in a lake of water from which he could never drink and to grasp at fruit that he could never reach.

A Hymn to Human Dignity

Although Zeus started out holding humans in contempt, over time he accepted their existence as a fact of life. He also sometimes stood as a model for justice, at least in the eyes of those Greeks who avidly worshipped him. In his play *Antigone*, the Athenian playwright Sophocles explored the theme of justice as it related to his fellow humans. The core of the play consists of the dramatic confrontation between the laws enacted by the state and society and those larger and more eternal natural laws, many of them enacted by the gods. All people have certain basic human rights, the author seems to say, including the right to a dignified burial, which is at first denied one of the play's main characters. Thus, *Antigone* stands as one of Western literature's great-est hymns to human worth and dignity, as well as a call for governments to honor these qualities, and the gods, too, with just laws. "Wonders there are many," sings the play's chorus,

> but none more wonderful than human beings. . . . Speech and wind-swift thought, and all the moods that create a community, they have taught themselves. . . . Cunning beyond the wildest of dreams is the skill that leads them, sometimes to evil, other times to good. As long as they honor the laws of the land and revere the justice of the gods, proudly their community will stand.

Sophocles. *Antigone* 368–406. Translated by the author.

Sophocles's play Antigone *is performed on stage in this modern production. The play explores dramatic confrontations between the laws of state and society and natural laws enacted by the gods.*

against one another. These included murder, betrayal, and various unnatural cruelties. The myths that depicted Tantalus's crime, his punishment, and the destruction of his descendants provided the Classical Greeks with a potent lesson. As expressed by the Athenian playwright Sophocles in his magnificent work *Antigone,* "There is no happiness where there is no wisdom," and there is "no wisdom but in submission to the gods."[32]

CHAPTER 5

Greek Mythology's Enormous Legacy

T he Greek myths were long associated with the ancient faith built around the Olympian gods, often called "Homeric religion," after the poet who first described those gods. That religion was strongest just before and during the first half of the Classical Age. Toward the end of that era and in the years that followed, however, Greek religious views steadily changed. Scholars Mark Morford and Robert Lenardon briefly summarize what happened:

> Anthropomorphic Homeric religion began to lose its force [and people] sought from religion not the civic self-confidence of Homeric cult, but comfort for their individual doubts and problems. [Over time], the legends of the gods ceased to be a vehicle for a living religion and became material for scholars. [They] were interested in explaining myths, and in so doing succeeded in explaining away the gods.[33]

Thus, during the last few centuries of ancient times (A.D. 100–500), when Greece was ruled by the Romans, many Greeks, especially educated ones, no longer believed that the heroes and other characters in the myths had been real. Nonetheless the stories survived the end of ancient times. In the medieval period that followed, scattered references to them appeared in Europe's folklore and art. Then, toward the end of medieval times, a much stronger interest in these tales emerged. In Morford and Lenardon's words, they enjoyed "a new lease on life that still endures."[34] Indeed, today the ancient Greek myths constitute one of the major legacies that the modern world has inherited from the ancient Greeks.

A Trend Toward Disbelief

The process by which the Greek myths ceased to be part of a living faith and became entertaining folktales began in a small way in the sixth century B.C. It was then that Greek scientists began to question traditional views of the universe, its structure, and humanity's place in nature. Logical, nonreligious explanations for the wonders of nature tended to make the mythical explanations for these wonders seem unnecessary. As scholar Sarah B. Pomeroy puts it,

> Mythology served the important function of grounding the growth of [the] cosmos from chaos in various actions taken by the gods. The great contribution of the sixth-century Greek thinkers [was] their determination to abandon this mythological and religious framework and attempt instead to explain the world by material processes alone.[35]

Another, larger blow to belief in the reality of the myths took the form of new approaches to education in the late fifth century B.C. The sophists, teachers who, for a price, dispensed "wisdom" about practical subjects, often tried to explain the gods and traditional myths as simply folk beliefs. There was a conservative social reaction to this trend by people worried about the demise of religion. That reaction culminated in the trial and execution of the Athenian philosopher Socrates in 399 B.C., partly for his supposed "atheism." Still, the damage had been done. In the following decades, intellectuals and educated people increasingly turned to philosophy instead of religion for guidance. Accordingly, mythology suffered. For example, Socrates's ardent pupil, the scholar-philosopher Plato, eliminated the Homeric legends from his ideal educational curriculum.

When Alexander the Great conquered the Middle East, Greek and Western ideas came in contact with Eastern ideas, customs, and religions. Many Greeks turned to these Eastern faiths for comfort.

Homeric religion and its cherished myths suffered still more in the late fourth century B.C. and the centuries that followed. The conquests of Alexander the Great brought Greece and its ideas into close contact with Eastern ideas, customs, and religions. Many Greeks turned to these Eastern practices for comfort, and the old Greek myths seemed more and more outmoded. The same thing happened on an even larger scale during the first centuries B.C. and A.D., when Eastern religions and cults spread to Rome, by this time master of the Greek lands. The Romans eagerly absorbed these foreign beliefs, often accepting them in place of the "state" religion, still presided over by the old Olympian gods (Jupiter, Mars, Minerva, and so forth).

Aiding this trend toward disbelief in the myths was the spread of literary scholarship in the Greco-Roman world. Thinkers and writers, including such intellectual giants as Callimachus, Apollonius of Rhodes, and Ovid, loved the old myths and retold them, often in great detail. But this was only for their entertainment value, as they and many of their readers did not think the events and characters in these stories were ever real.

Even more important for the way future generations viewed these myths was that Classical Greek thinkers frequently attempted to explain where the myths had come from, just as modern experts do. Especially influential in this regard was Euhemerus, a fourth-century B.C. Greek who suggested that the traditional gods were originally human rulers and military heroes. Over time, he said, they came to be seen as more powerful than they had actually been and thereby gained divine status.

Medieval Survival of the Myths

The final blow against the old myths in ancient times was the rise of Christianity. That faith became Rome's official religion in the late 300s A.D., and worship of the traditional Greco-Roman gods was banned. Many Greek and Roman pagans (non-Christians) carried on their rituals in private. True, they no longer thought that the old tales had any basis in fact, but they retained and passed on those myths. This is because they saw them as part of their cultural heritage, in the same way that many modern people, Christians and non-Christians alike, view folktales like Noah's ark as crucial components of their own cultural background.

Yet the pagans were not the only ones who perpetuated the Greek myths. After the western Roman Empire disintegrated in the fifth and sixth centuries A.D., the Christian church survived and became Europe's spiritual guide. Over time, Christian thinkers and writers frequently used the old pagan tales,

It's in the Stars

Some of the ancient Greek myths survived in the belief system of astrology, which associates various constellations in the sky with mythical characters. For example, the constellation now called Gemini, the Twins, was thought to depict the brothers Castor and Pollux, who sailed with Jason on the quest for the Golden Fleece.

Augustine Dismisses the Greek Gods

The Greek scholar Euhemerus ended up doing his countrymen and their beliefs a disservice when he said that the gods were originally real historical characters of the dim past rather than divine beings. In the fourth and fifth centuries, when Christianity gained prominence in Rome, Christian writers used what had come to be called "Euhemerism" to attack the pagan gods. The fourth-century A.D. Christian writer Augustine, for example, wrote,

Afar more credible account of these gods is given, when it is said that they were men, and that to each one of them sacred rites and solemnities were instituted, according to his particular genius, manners, actions, circumstances . . . the poets adorning them with lies, and false spirits seducing men to receive them. For it far more likely that some youth . . .

The fourth-century A.D. Christian writer Augustine attacked and discredited the pagan gods and derided pagan beliefs.

being desirous to reign, dethroned his father, than that . . . Saturn [Cronus] was overthrown by his son, Jupiter.

Augustine. *The City of God.* Translated by Marcus Dods. Chicago: Encyclopedia Britannica, 1952, p. 254.

sometimes to teach a moral lesson, and at other times to make their own stories sound more romantic. Comparing a character or animal to a counterpart in Greek mythology became a way to add a colorful literary flourish. Medieval writers also kept the old myths alive by continuing to associate many of the constellations in the night sky with mythical characters.

In this way, many Greek myths were literally woven into the fabric of medieval Western culture. This, in turn, led to a big revival of interest in them in the Renaissance, the great flowering of literature and the arts that occurred in the last two or so medieval centuries (c. 1300–c. 1550). The Roman writer Ovid, whose *Metamorphoses* had been one of the most comprehensive ancient collections of Greco-Roman myths, became particularly popular among Renaissance writers. They took his tellings of those tales and reworked them just enough to get across their own moral points or lessons. One of the major examples of this trend was the *Ovide Moralisé,* a fourteenth-century French work. Among other things, it claimed that the Greek nymph Daphne, known for her virginity, was actually a disguised version of the Virgin Mary.

The Renaissance was also known for its many gifted painters, and some of them used events and characters from the Greek myths for subjects. One of the best-known examples is *The Birth of Venus,* a painting by the fifteenth-century Italian artist Sandro Botticelli. It shows the goddess, known as Aphrodite to the Greeks, standing in a huge scallop shell, having just risen from the sea foam churned up by the battle between Uranus and his son Cronus.

Among the other Italian Renaissance painters who prominently dealt with mythological subjects were Giovanni Bellini and Tiziano Vecellio, better known as Titian. One of Titian's greatest works, *Bacchus and Ariadne,* completed in 1524, shows the beautiful young woman Ariadne, who has just been abandoned on an island by the Athenian hero Theseus. Bacchus (the Roman version of Dionysus, god of the grapevine and of fertility) is leaping toward her from his chariot, having fallen in love with her at first sight. This magnificent work now hangs in London's National Gallery. Titian and Bellini collaborated on another masterpiece, *The Feast of the Gods.* (Bellini started the work in 1514 but died two years later, after which Titian stepped in and finished it.) The canvas, which depicts several of the Olympian gods in the midst of a picnic, is now in the National Gallery of Art in Washington, D.C.

Still another late Renaissance artist who was inspired by Greek mythology was a German named Albrecht Dürer. One of his best-known works, the *Sky-Map of the Northern*

The Ovide Moralisé *is a fourteenth-century French rendition of Ovid's* Metamorphoses, *shown here. Renaissance writers reworked the old Greek myths to get across their own moral lessons.*

Hemisphere, was finished in 1515. It depicts a huge circle representing the night sky, including the major constellations, which are shown in the forms of characters and animals from the myths. Among them are the flying horse Pegasus; the hero Perseus holding the hideous head of the snake-haired Medusa; and another renowned hero, Heracles, who swings one of his symbols, a club.

Early Modern Mythical Allusions

Steeped in the Greek myths thanks to their wide use in the Renaissance, early modern writers, painters, and other artists also incorporated these stories into their works. Especially prolific among the writers in this regard were several Englishmen. The seventeenth-century English poet John Milton, for instance, included more than thirty allusions (references or quotations) from mythology in his short poem *Comus* alone. Milton's renowned epic poem *Paradise Lost* (1667) contains hundreds of such allusions.

Even Milton's liberal use of references to the Greek myths paled in comparison with that of the sixteenth-century English playwright William Shakespeare. Indeed, entire books have been penned about Shakespeare's mythological allusions, which number in the thousands. Some were direct; in a single speech from *Hamlet,* for instance, the title character compares his mother with Niobe, the mythical woman who was punished by the deities Apollo and Artemis for disrespecting them; his dead father with the Greek sun god Hyperion; and himself (unfavorably) with the hero Hercules (the Roman name for Heracles), as well as mentioning a satyr, a mythical Greek creature that was half-man and half-goat.

Shakespeare also skillfully utilized the Greek myths in more indirect ways. His much-beloved play *Romeo and Juliet,* written in the 1590s, is a good example. He based the story on English poet Arthur Brooke's 1562 poem *The Tragical History of Romeus and Juliet*; yet Brooke had not been completely original either. He had based that poem on earlier French and Italian works that, in their turn, were based partly on Ovid's telling of the Greek myth of Pyramis and Thisbe. Just as Juliet took her own life when she found her lover Romeo's apparently dead body, Thisbe stabbed herself to death on seeing Pyramis's lifeless form. In Ovid's words, Thisbe, holding the knife, cries out, "Only death could have separated you from

Homage to Antigone

Of the numerous plays, operas, and other modern works based on the myth of Antigone, one of the more unusual was a 2004 album, *Antigone,* by the German heavy metal band Heaven Shall Burn. Among the album's songs are "The Weapon They Fear" and "The Only Truth."

William Shakespeare made many allusions to Greek myths in his plays. His Romeo and Juliet *was based partly on the Greek myth of Pyramis and Thisbe, two lovers who also met a tragic suicidal end.*

me, but not even death will part us!"[36] (Shakespeare also used the tale of Pyramis and Thisbe more directly in his play *A Midsummer Night's Dream* in the scene in which a group of simple folk meet in the woods to rehearse their version of a play based on that old myth.)

Music Based on Myths

No less fruitfully than writers and artists, musical composers—from early modern times up to the present—have created a wealth of wonderful works based on the Greco-Roman myths. The first examples were operas, a musical genre that was extremely popular in Europe from the 1600s through the 1800s. In fact, one of the earliest known operas was *Euridice,* inspired by the myth of Orpheus and Eurydice, in which Orpheus disobeyed Hades, causing his beloved wife to remain forever in the Underworld.

In 1858 French composer Hector Berlioz produced The Trojans, *an opera based on the Roman writer Virgil's account. Here, it is performed in modern-day France.*

First performed in 1600 at the marriage of two leading nobles, *Euridice* was created by composer Jacopo Peri and other members of the Camerata, an artistic society based in Florence, Italy. Peri sang the part of Orpheus himself and helped to establish opera as a popular new artistic medium combining visual spectacle and complex, descriptive musical numbers.

Other popular operas based on mythical subjects followed. One, *Jason* (1649), by Italy's Pier Francesco Cavalli, depicted the familiar story of the quest for the Golden Fleece by the Argonauts, a group of heroes led by Jason. In 1767, German composer Christoph Willibald Gluck, premiered *Iphigenia in Aulis,* taken from the Trojan Cycle of myths. In it, Agamemnon despairs that the Greek fleet bound for Troy cannot set sail because of a lack of wind. To get the goddess Artemis to provide the winds needed, he sacrifices his own daughter, Iphigenia. (Later, Agamemnon pays dearly for this act when his wife, Clytemnestra, murders him.) French composer Hector Berlioz also produced an opera based on the exploits of a Trojan hero—*The Trojans* (1858), in this case as told by the great Roman writer Virgil.

Many other musical forms besides opera proved themselves highly effective in portraying mythical stories and characters in entertaining ways. A particularly popular form that emerged in the twentieth century was the American Broadway musical. It typically consists of a play in which the characters not only speak dialogue but also break into song at appropriate points in the story.

A notable early example was Richard Rodgers and Lorenz Hart's *By Jupiter* (1942), based on one of the legendary exploits of the Greek strongman Heracles. In a lighthearted approach, the dialogue and music tell how the hero goes on a long journey to bring back the magical girdle (belt) of the queen of the Amazons, a mythical race of warrior women. (The quest for the girdle was one of Heracles's famous twelve labors. In a fit of madness maliciously caused by the goddess Hera, the usually heroic Heracles kills his wife and children. Seeking forgiveness, he travels to Delphi, where the famous oracle advises him to put himself in the service of King Eurystheus of Tiryns for twelve years. Eurystheus makes Heracles perform twelve superhuman labors, including killing a rampaging lion, capturing the fearsome Cretan bull, and acquiring the girdle of Hippolyta, queen of the Amazons.)

Perhaps the most renowned and beloved Broadway show based on the Greek myths is Alan Jay Lerner's and Frederick Loewe's *My Fair Lady* (1956), which featured a young Julie Andrews in the original cast. The script was taken from English playwright George Bernard Shaw's 1913 play *Pygmalion.* Shaw had loosely based his play on the story of Pygmalion and Galatea, as told by Ovid. In that tale, Pygmalion is a sculptor who carves a statue of a beautiful woman, falls in love with it, and wishes that it could somehow come to life. Aphrodite and her son Eros overhear that wish and transform the statue into a woman named Galatea, whom Pygmalion marries. In both Shaw's play and the Broadway musical version, the Pygmalion character is Professor Henry Higgins, a prim and proper Englishman who teaches phonetics. He manages to change an uncultured, poor-mannered woman of the streets, Eliza Doolittle, into a proper lady who is accepted into respectable society. Also, as the story unfolds, the teacher and his pupil fall in love.

Stories Alive on the Screen

The twentieth century also introduced a new art form that combines aspects of many others, including writing, visual composition, theatrical elements, and music, among others. This all-encompassing art form is the motion picture. From the silent era on into the sound era of film, it was clear that movies could retell the ancient tales in ways that the written word, paintings, musical works, and even stage plays could not. A film could reenact the events of a myth using actors in realistic settings. That made the story seem to be literally alive on the screen in a highly dramatic and entertaining manner.

More than a hundred movies dealing directly with Greek mythology have been made so far. Among the earliest was the silent film *Ulysses and the Giant Polyphemus,* made in France in 1905. (Ulysses was the Roman name for the Greek hero Odysseus.) It was the first of several films to re-create scenes from Homer's *Odyssey.* Also tackling Homer was a 1911 Italian film, *The Fall of Troy,* which was extremely ambitious for its day. Hundreds of extras were used for the scene in which the Trojans pull the wooden horse into their city. Film historian Jon Solomon writes,

> Although it was considered a "spectacular" in 1911, this primitive, brief, and low-budget film seems humorous and crude today. But at the turn of the century, when films about the ancient world were at one of the peaks of their popularity, the excitement about seeing the Trojan Horse, Helen, and Paris on the screen for the first time overcame the [film's] technical inadequacies.[37]

Several other movies dealing with the Trojan War followed, including two big-budget versions. One was the 1956 Warner Brothers version, *Helen of Troy,* directed by Robert Wise; the other was the 2004 extravaganza *Troy,* starring Brad Pitt as Achilles. Though both were entertaining, neither was very faithful to the myths told in Homer's *Iliad* and the other epics in the ancient Trojan Cycle.

Considerably more effective in capturing the other-worldly, quaint, and at times fantastic atmosphere of Greek mythology was the 1963 American film *Jason and the Argonauts.* A loose rendition of the *Argonautica,* an epic poem by Apollonius of Rhodes, the movie is notable for two achievements. One is its excellent, Homeric-style portrayal of Zeus and the other gods as enormous, powerful entities lounging in their palaces on Mount Olympus and glancing down with disdain at the tiny humans far below.

The other outstanding aspect of the film is its special-effects wizardry, accomplished by Ray Harryhausen, the great master of stop-motion animation. That process, which has largely been replaced by digital animation, utilizes realistic-looking miniature models that are animated one frame at a time. The movie's scenes of the Argonauts fighting an incredible array of mythical monsters, including skeletons and the drag-

Mixing Mythologies

Both film versions of *Clash of the Titans* deal with the Greek hero Perseus and his killing of the snake-haired monster Medusa. However, they also feature a giant sea monster, the Kraken, which comes from some old Norwegian and Icelandic myths rather than Greek mythology.

on guarding the Golden Fleece, remain marvels of both the filmmaking art and modern re-creations of the Greek myths. "Harryhausen's genius takes our impression of the Greek mythological world into a new dimension of visual reality,"[38] Solomon remarks.

In the decades that followed *Jason and the Argonauts*, a number of other major motion pictures about the Greek myths were made. These included two versions of *Clash of the Titans* (in 1981 and 2010), about the adventures of the hero Perseus. Several big-budget TV miniseries also appeared, prominent among them *The Odyssey* (1997), a remake of *Jason and the Argonauts* (2000), and *Hercules* (2005). The latter was still another in a line of at least thirty films about the muscular hero Heracles. In addition, a strong appeal was made to young people with *Percy Jackson and the Olympians: The Lightning Thief* (2010), based on a series of young-adult books by Rick Riordan.

Jason battles the skeletons in the 1963 film Jason and the Argonauts. *Loosely based on the* Argonautica, *it is one of the most popular films based on Greek myths.*

A Mine of Images and Symbols

Movies and television are important forms of pop culture. Among many others are TV commercials; company names on billboards and television; names of popular sports teams, theaters, cars, and a wide range of consumer products; and colorful logos representing various companies. All of these aspects of modern culture have long been fertile ground for references to Greek mythology. This may be partly because the companies who choose these product names and logos are aware that the old myths, or at least visual images and symbols based on them, have become ingrained in society's subconscious. That is, certain images from the myths are automatically recognized by nearly everyone.

Examples of such myth-based pop-culture names are everywhere. Some of the car names include the Saturn (the Roman name for the Titan Cronus), Honda's minivan the Odyssey (named for Homer's epic), Toyota's Echo (named for a Greek nymph who starved herself to death), and

Examples of Greek myth–based pop culture names abound in today's culture. From Odyssey minivans and Olympus cameras to Poseidon missiles and Nike shoes, to name a few, the Greek myths have left a cultural legacy in our modern world.

The Myths On the "Silver Screen"

Jon Solomon, a professor of classics at the University of Arizona, here explains why the Greek myths are such popular subjects for movies.

When the immortal Homer sang his glorious poems just shy of three thousand years ago, he could not possibly have imagined that someday his poems about Odysseus, Achilles, and the Trojan War would be recreated on something called a "silver screen." But the twentieth century A.D. still found the whole fabulous world of Greek mythology captivating, and it would have been unwise for movie producers to have left this magical source of heroes and monsters untapped. For centuries the gloriously mysterious atmosphere surrounding such names as Helen, Troy, Perseus, Hercules, Jason, Orpheus, and Medusa created indelible impressions on the minds and eyes of artists. Those impressions were bound to emerge in the ultimate artistic medium of the Atomic Age. [That medium, film] made these vivid legends of ancient Greece popular enough to live on two millennia after the peoples that fostered them have perished.

Jon Solomon. *The Ancient World in the Cinema.* New Haven: Yale University Press, 2001, pp. 101-102.

Buick's Electra (named for King Agamemnon's daughter). Among the well-known company names are Midas Muffler (after the mythical character whose touch turned objects into gold), sportswear giant Nike, Inc. (named for the Greek goddess of victory), Olympus cameras (after the abode of the gods), Orion Pictures (named after a mythical giant hunter whom the gods placed in the night sky), and Amazon.com (after the mythical race of warrior women). Only a few of the products named for Greek mythological figures or objects include Ajax cleanser (named for a powerful warrior in Homer's *Iliad*), Trident gum (after the symbol wielded by the sea god Poseidon), and Hermès handbags (a French designer's tribute to the Greek messenger god). This list—a very brief one—of popular companies and products based on Greek myths, demonstrates the degree to which those tales have been woven into the fabric of Western civilization.

Consider, in addition, the many plays, books, paintings, musical pieces, movies, graphic novels, computer games, and other genres that have been inspired by the myths. Clearly, the survival of the Greek myths constitutes a cultural legacy of enormous proportions. As a result, the great civilization that created these stories is gone only in the flesh-and-blood sense. It remains very much alive in the art, architecture, literature, philosophy, and especially the body of myths it handed down to future generations. Morford and Lenardon write,

> The Classical myths have not died [because] their literary tradition is too strong and their beauty too great for them to be dispensable [unneeded]. Even where they are not found to be beautiful or noble, they remain an inexhaustible mine of image and symbol. . . . Even the briefest survey cannot help but forcibly remind us [of] the potent inspiration that [Greek] mythology provides for all facets of creative artistic expression.[39]

NOTES

Introduction: Products of Ancient Imagination

1. Michael Grant. *Myths of the Greeks and Romans.* New York: Plume, 1995, pp. xvii–xviii.
2. Edith Hamilton. *Mythology.* New York: Grand Central, 1999, p. 13.
3. Grant. *Myths of the Greeks and Romans,* p. xix.

Chapter 1: Myths as Memories

4. C.M. Bowra. *Classical Greece.* New York: Time-Life, 1977, p. 12.
5. Sarah B. Pomeroy et al. *Ancient Greece: A Political, Social, and Cultural History.* New York: Oxford University Press, 2007, pp. 1–3.
6. Quoted in Rhoda A. Hendricks, ed. and trans. *Classical Gods and Heroes: Myths as Told by the Ancient Authors.* New York: Morrow Quill, 1974, pp. 33–34.
7. C.M. Bowra. *The Greek Experience.* New York: Barnes and Noble, 1996, p. 32.
8. Michael Grant. *The Rise of the Greeks.* New York: Scribner's, 2006, p. 17.
9. Pindar. *Pindar: The Odes.* Translated by C.M. Bowra. New York: Penguin, 1985, p. 206.

10. Quoted in Hendricks. *Classical Gods and Heroes,* p. 77.
11. Hamilton. *Mythology,* p. 20.

Chapter 2: Stories About Creation

12. W.H.D. Rouse. *Gods, Heroes and Men of Ancient Greece.* New York: New American Library, 2001, p. 11.
13. Rouse. *Gods, Heroes and Men of Ancient Greece,* p. 11.
14. Hamilton. *Mythology,* p. 65.
15. Rodney Castleden. *Minoans: Life in Bronze Age Crete.* New York: Routledge, 1993, p. 59.
16. Rouse. *Gods, Heroes and Men of Ancient Greece,* p. 18.
17. Bowra. *The Greek Experience,* p. 67.

Chapter 3: The Heroes of Troy and Other Champions

18. Grant. *Myths of the Greeks and Romans,* pp. 45–46.
19. Quoted in Arrian. *Anabasis Alexandri* 5.26. translated by the author.
20. Euripides. *Euripides: Alcestis, Hippolytus, Iphigenia in Tauris.* Translated by Philip Vellacott. Baltimore: Penguin, 1974, p. 147.

21. Homer. *Iliad.* Translated by E.V. Rieu. Baltimore: Penguin, 1989, p. 400.
22. Homer. *Iliad,* p. 406.
23. Virgil. *The Aeneid.* Translated by Patric Dickinson. New York: New American Library, 2002, p. 29.
24. Homer. *Odyssey.* Translated by E.V. Rieu. Baltimore: Penguin, 1987, p. 147.
25. Quoted in Thucydides. *The Peloponnesian War.* Translated by Rex Warner. New York: Penguin, 2008, p. 149.

Chapter 4: The Will of the Gods

26. Bowra. *The Greek Experience,* p. 69.
27. Ovid. *Metamorphoses.* Translated by Rolfe Humphries. Bloomington: Indiana University Press, 1967, p. 201.
28. Quoted in Hendricks. *Classical Gods and Heroes,* p. 72.
29. Hesiod. *Works and Days.* In *Hesiod and Theognis.* Translated by Dorothea Wender. New York: Penguin, 1973, p. 61.
30. Quoted in Hendricks. *Classical Gods and Heroes,* p. 25.
31. Homer. *Odyssey.* Translated by W.H.D. Rouse. New York: Signet, 2007, p. 136.
32. Sophocles. *Antigone.* In *The Oedipus Cycle,* edited and translated by Dudley Fitts and Robert Fitzgerald. New York: Harcourt Brace, 1997, pp. 235, 238.

Chapter 5: Greek Mythology's Enormous Legacy

33. Mark P.O. Morford and Robert J. Lenardon. *Classical Mythology.* New York: Oxford University Press, 2010, pp. 462–464.
34. Morford and Lenardon. *Classical Mythology,* p. 468.
35. Pomeroy et al. *Ancient Greece,* p. 258.
36. Ovid. *Metamorphoses.* Translated by Mary M. Innes. New York: Penguin, 2006, p. 98.
37. Jon Solomon. *The Ancient World in the Cinema.* New Haven, CT: Yale University Press, 2001, p. 103.
38. Solomon. *The Ancient World in the Cinema,* p. 115.
39. Morford and Lenardon. *Classical Mythology,* pp. 476, 491.

anthropomorphism: Assigning human attributes to animals, inanimate objects, or natural forces (gods).

aoidoi: In ancient Greece, roving minstrels, bards, or storytellers.

arete: A combination of moral excellence and warlike valor held as the ideal ancient Greek virtue.

bronze: An alloy, or mixture, of the metals copper and tin.

classics: Academic subjects pertaining to ancient Greek and Roman culture.

cosmos: The Greek word for the ordered universe.

cult: In ancient times, a religious congregation or other group whose members devoted themselves to a certain god.

cult image: A statue of a god, usually placed in a temple or other important religious venue.

cycle: A collection of related myths, often called a saga.

epic poem: A long literary work, in verse, with larger-than-life characters and serious themes such as war, heroism, and human destiny.

oracle: A message believed to come from the gods; the sacred site where such a message was given; or the person who delivers the message.

prophecy: A prediction about future events.

sacrifice: An offering made to satisfy a god or gods.

sanctuary: In ancient Greece, a sacred area made up of a temple and its surrounding grounds.

sophist: "Wise man"; in ancient Greece, a traveling teacher who charged a fee for his services.

Titanomachy: The mythical battle between the Titans and Olympians for control of the universe.

trident: A three-pronged spear, similar to a pitchfork, famous as the symbol of the sea god Poseidon.

Books

David Bellingham. *An Introduction to Greek Mythology.* Secaucus, NJ: Chartwell Books, 2002. This book explains the major Greek myths and legends and their importance to the ancient Greeks and contains many beautiful photos and drawings.

Peter Connolly. *The Legend of Odysseus.* New York: Oxford University Press, 2005. This is an excellent, easy-to-read summary of the events of Homer's *Iliad* and *Odyssey,* including many informative sidebars about the way people lived in Mycenaean times. Also contains many stunning illustrations of ships, fortresses, homes, weapons, and armor of that age.

Kathleen N. Daly. *Greek and Roman Mythology A to Z.* New York: Chelsea House, 2009. This useful summary of major myths and mythical characters is aimed at young adult readers.

J. Lesley Fitton. *The Discovery of the Greek Bronze Age.* Cambridge, MA: Harvard University Press, 2001. Fitton does an excellent job of reporting the known facts about Greece's Bronze Age and the modern archaeological discoveries relating to that turbulent period.

Michael Grant. *Myths of the Greeks and Romans.* New York: Plume, 1995. One of the twentieth century's most prolific ancient historians delivers a very readable and enlightening study of the major Greek and Roman myths.

Michael Grant. *The Rise of the Greeks.* New York: Macmillan, 1987. In this excellent book, Grant explains how Greek civilization arose, including the manner in which real events and people later became the models for the events and characters of various myths.

Michael Grant and John Hazel. *Who's Who in Classical Mythology.* London: Routledge, 2002. This resource is the most comprehensive overview of the events and characters of Greek and Roman mythology. The entries are clearly written and easy to follow.

Roger L. Green. *Tales of the Greek Heroes.* London: Puffin, 2009. Several famous Greek myths are retold here for younger readers.

Zachery Hamby. *Mythology for Teens: Classic Myths for Today's World.* Austin, TX: Prufrock Press, 2009. This attractive, well-written presentation of some of the Greek myths will appeal to young readers.

Edith Hamilton. *Mythology*. New York: Grand Central, 1999. Hamilton's excellent retelling of the Greek myths is still considered by many to be the most entertaining overview of its kind.

Rhoda A. Hendricks, ed. and trans. *Classical Gods and Heroes: Myths as Told by the Ancient Authors*. New York: Morrow Quill, 1974. This is a very useful collection of easy-to-read translations of famous Greek myths and tales, as told by ancient Greek and Roman writers.

Homer. *Iliad*. Translated by E.V. Rieu. Baltimore: Penguin, 1989. This is one of the better translations of Homer's great tale of Achilles and the exploits of the other heroes of the Trojan War.

Homer. *Odyssey*. Translated by E.V. Rieu. Baltimore: Penguin, 1987. Rieu also does a fine job with Homer's other classic epic, which tells about Odysseus's adventures in the years following the war at Troy.

Mark P.O. Morford and Robert J. Lenardon. *Classical Mythology*. New York: Oxford University Press, 2010. This well-written volume features background and analysis of the major Greek and Roman myths, as well as a section on the legacy of those stories in later ages.

Ovid. *Metamorphoses*. Translated by Mary M. Innes. New York: Penguin, 2006. Ovid's collection of myths, compiled in the opening years of the Roman Empire, contains brief but enlightening versions of nearly all the major Greek myths.

W.H.D. Rouse. *Gods, Heroes and Men of Ancient Greece*. New York: New American Library, 2001. This is a colorfully written, enjoyable romp through the classic Greek myths by the late Rouse, who was a great teacher, translator, and writer.

Sophocles. *Oedipus the King*. Translated by Bernard M.W. Knox. New York: Simon and Schuster, 2005. This is one of the best translations of this play, which remains as powerful and shocking as it was when Sophocles wrote it more than twenty-four centuries ago.

Michael Stapleton. *The Illustrated Dictionary of Greek and Roman Mythology*. New York: Peter Bedrick, 1988. This volume remains one of the best introductions to Greek mythology, thanks to its lively, easy-to-read text and outstanding illustrations.

Rex Warner. *Men and Gods*. New York: NYRB, 2008. This is a spellbinding retelling of thirty-eight Greek myths by a great scholar and storyteller, whom one literary critic called "an outstanding novelist of ideas."

Philip Wilkinson, *The Illustrated Dictionary of Mythology*. New York: Dorling Kindersley, 2006. Like other Dorling Kindersley books, this one contains many beautiful illustrations, which go well with the easy-to-read stories of mythical characters.

Internet Sources

Greek Mythology Link. "Achilles." www .maicar.com/GML/Achilles.html.

A very detailed presentation of this important mythical character.

Greek Mythology Link. "Helen." www.maicar.com/GML/Helen.html. A long, fascinating description of the great beauty who was said to have had "the face that launched a thousand ships."

Greek Mythology Link. "Oedipus." www.maicar.com/GML/Oedipus.html. A terrific, detailed article about one of the most important, and most tragic, characters in Greek mythology.

Richard Hooker. "Homer." www.wsu.edu:8080/~dee/MINOA/HOMER.HTM. A very informative overview of the famous Greek bard by a noted scholar at Washington State University.

Richard Hooker. "Polyphemos." www.wsu.edu:8080/~dee/MINOA/POLY.HTM. Teacher and writer Hooker tells the absorbing, sometimes frightening tale of Odysseus's encounter with the man-eating, one-eyed giant.

Theoi Greek Mythology. "Apollo." www.theoi.com/Olympios/Apollon.html. Contains practically everything one might need to know about this key Olympian god, the most versatile of the Greek deities.

Theoi Greek Mythology. "The Titans." www.theoi.com/greek-mythology/titans.html. A fact-filled synopsis of the members of the first race of Greek gods.

Websites

Homer's *Iliad* and *Odyssey* (http://library.thinkquest.org/19300/data/homer.htm). Click on the links titled "Iliad," then on "Virtual Iliad," and "Odyssey" and then "Virtual Odyssey," which lead to detailed overviews of the stories of these classic epics.

Theoi Greek Mythology (www.theoi.com). The site (*theoi* means "gods" in Greek) with the most comprehensive and reliable general source for Greek mythology on the Internet.

INDEX

PICTURE CREDITS

ABOUT THE AUTHOR

Historian Don Nardo has written numerous acclaimed volumes about ancient civilizations and peoples. Among these are studies of the religious beliefs and myths of those peoples, including the Greeks, Romans, Egyptians, and Sumerians, as well as others. Mr. Nardo also composes and arranges orchestral music. He resides with his wife, Christine, in Massachusetts.